"*Design + Anthropology* represents an important n
and important field of artistic and intellectual inquiry.... Both anthropologists
and designers will read this book with great advantage."

Allen W. Batteau, Wayne State University, USA

"Miller masterfully illuminates the territory between anthropology and design
by weaving together a wide range of voices into a rich narrative.... An essential
read for anyone interested in the intersection of anthropology and design."

Christina Wasson, University of North Texas, USA

"In this highly relevant book, Christine Miller bridges the gap between designers
and anthropologists, describing how to create collaborative innovation networks
to build interdisciplinary pathways between the yin and yang of innovation."

Peter A. Gloor, Massachusetts Institute of Technology (MIT), USA

DESIGN + ANTHROPOLOGY

This book explores the evolution of two disciplines, design and anthropology, and their convergence within commercial and organizational arenas. Focusing on the transdisciplinary field of design anthropology, the chapters cover the global forces and conditions that facilitated its emergence, the people that have contributed to its development and those who are likely to shape its future. Christine Miller touches on the invention and diffusion of new practices, the recontextualization of ethnographic inquiry within design and innovations in applications of anthropological theory and methodology. She considers how encounters between anthropology and 'designerly' practice have impacted the evolution of both disciplines. The book provides students, scholars and practitioners with valuable insight into the movement to formalize the nascent field of design anthropology and how the relationship between the two fields might develop in the future given the dynamic global forces that continue to impact them both.

Christine Miller is Clinical Associate Professor of Innovation in the Stuart School of Business at the Illinois Institute of Technology, USA. Her research interests incorporate how sociality and culture influence the design and diffusion of new products, processes, and technologies. She studies technology-mediated communication and knowledge work flows within multiple discipline groups, teams, and networks and the emergence of collaborative innovation networks (COINs).

DESIGN + ANTHROPOLOGY

Converging Pathways in Anthropology and Design

Christine Miller

Routledge
Taylor & Francis Group

NEW YORK AND LONDON

First published 2018
by Routledge
711 Third Avenue, New York, NY 10017

and by Routledge
2 Park Square, Milton Park, Abingdon, Oxon OX14 4RN

Routledge is an imprint of the Taylor & Francis Group, an informa business

British Library Cataloguing-in-Publication Data
A catalogue record for this book is available from the British Library

Library of Congress Cataloging-in-Publication Data
Names: Miller, Christine (Christine Z.)
Title: Design + anthropology: converging pathways in
anthropology and design / Christine Miller.
Other titles: Design and anthropology
Description: Abingdon, Oxon; New York, NY: Routledge, 2017. |
Includes bibliographical references and index.
Identifiers: LCCN 2017016780 | ISBN 9781629583181
(hardback: alk. paper) | ISBN 9781629583198 (pbk.: alk. paper) |
ISBN 9781315101903 (ebook)
Subjects: LCSH: Design—Anthropological aspects. |
Design—Human factors. | Art and anthropology. | Art and design.
Classification: LCC NK1520 .M55 2017 | DDC 745.4—dc23
LC record available at https://lccn.loc.gov/2017016780

ISBN: 978-1-629-58318-1 (hbk)
ISBN: 978-1-629-58319-8 (pbk)
ISBN: 978-1-315-10190-3 (ebk)

Typeset in Bembo
by codeMantra

To Dave Miller, my husband and collaborator

CONTENTS

FIGURES AND TABLES

Figures

Tables

FOREWORD

Timothy de Waal Malefyt, Series Editor

A Better Designed Anthropology: Crafting a More Enlightened Innovation Process

Business anthropology is an emergent and hybrid discipline (Baba, 2006) that is still in a *process of becoming* (Ingold, 2013). This hybrid discipline is rapidly ascending, in part, because of the growth of design anthropology – a main source of marketplace innovation. Design anthropology, we learn from Christine Miller's enlightening book, bridges an anthropological focus with design studies in ways that use the anthropologist's unique ability to "look beneath" consumer practices, uncover deeper motivations, and link these insights back to improve consumer – product interactions that organizations find useful. Design *and* anthropology, while independent disciplines, have merged to elevate the growth of design anthropology because their capabilities "correspond" (Ingold, 2013) in mutually enhancing ways. This new work by Christine Miller thoughtfully traces these entanglements through histories and future potentialities that have led to the emergence of design anthropology. This emergence occurred, we learn, only because vast changes in anthropology, design studies, and capitalism paved the way for this fruitful convergence. I briefly trace these developments and how this juncture informs innovating opportunities that design anthropology offers corporations, business anthropologists, and beyond.

As Miller traces in her chapters, a "turn" of events occurred in the 1980s and 1990s in the field of anthropology, when the study of culture and the consumption of goods and services were no longer viewed as a detriment to culture, but rather offered an enlightened outlook. Newer investigations acknowledged consumption as the very means by which consumers expressed their creativity and diversity (Baba, 2006). Anthropologist Daniel Miller (1995, 1997, 2005) contends that consumption and material culture is the contemporary means by which people demonstrate their cultural identities and relate to one another. Against earlier admonitions of the growing threat of mass-market coercion and capitalistic manipulation (Horkheimer & Adorno, 1969; see also Klein, 2000), consumers under newer anthropological investigations were revealed to be "interpretive agents" who sought to form "lifestyles that defy dominant consumerist norms or that directly challenge corporate power" (Arnould & Thompson, 2005: 875). Consumers were no longer considered "passive dupes" (Sherry, 2008: 90), but recast as active agents and worthy subjects of investigation. Many businesses at this juncture also changed from a product-marketing focus to a consumer-marketing focus, placing the agentive consumer at the center of the marketing equation (Kotler & Armstrong, 2016). In this context, the role of research anthropologist also shifted from passive observer and interpreter of social structure, to an active agent and willing participant in the network that helped move along social and cultural change.

Likewise, we learn that design studies experienced a rebirth and a coming into its own, shifting from previous object-centered "form givers" and simply "makers" of products (Owen, 2006) to consumer-focused *interventionists*. Designers of brands, products, and services became major players in the new capitalist agenda of innovation and future-making (Thrift, 2005). Participatory design, as Miller details, not only "requires creating new ways to draw out and articulate 'the possible,' but also to explore ways to facilitate and guide dynamic transformative action." Designers are now intervening in increasingly complex situations of multidimensional contexts that involve social, cultural, environmental, economic, political, and technological factors. We further learn from Miller that design practice now includes awareness and debates on how best to prepare young designers to address variable situations that involve not only a concern for "the user" of a specific product or service (i.e., human-centered design), but also systems-level concerns about the impact of designed artifacts on people, the environment, and society. At the forefront of these concerns are design anthropologists who help bring about and embrace vast technological, innovative, and environmental changes in the world aided by new tools and methods of analysis. Design innovation and consumer engagement are then informative ways that design anthropologists are impacting capitalistic practices and consumer markets as their *modus operandi* for change. They accomplish this by embracing new technologies, innovation imperatives, and coconsumer efforts discussed below.

First, design anthropologists help integrate new technologies and ways of understanding them in the consumer marketplace, such as the introduction of Big Data, the deployment of sensors, smart phones, and other electronic devices, which inform ways to better serve institutions and consumer interactions. The "aestheticisation of everyday life" has arrived where increasingly the "look and feel" of things, matter (Featherstone, 2007). Sensory appeals in design are everywhere, "...they are increasingly personalized and they are intensifying" (Postrel, 2003: 5). Samsung and other consumer goods firms have achieved marketing success by redesigning home TVs, for example, not as smart electronic devices, but as aesthetically "designed furniture" (Madsbjerg & Rasmussen, 2014: 155–157). Design anthropologists also help data analysts refigure Big Data's relevance; not for its unimaginable calculative abilities, but for the way factual numbers are transformed into and interpret consumer subjectivities. Big Data brings about an "enchantment" to modernity in how it "creates meaning out of chaos, tells compelling stories, and forecasts the future" (Malefyt, 2017: 2). Microsoft analysts then use technology not for its speed and size, but for its relationality to revealing other data and people. As business anthropologists Dana Boyd and Kate Crawford note, "Big Data is highly social even if the illusion of science is intellectual" (Boyd & Crawford, 2011: 1). This is another way that designers and anthropologists collaborate to help understand social patterns and innovate by making empirical connections between other data, groups of people, or simply the structure of information itself.

Second, design anthropologists are also at the forefront of innovation as a global business imperative. They continually experiment with new perspectives on field research, improvise new methods and frameworks of analysis, and synthesize new theory as it emerges from raw data. As capitalism seeks ever-changing forms of networks, innovation is viewed as essential to corporate growth, economic prosperity, and even social well-being (Ingold & Hallam, 2007: 1). The innovative design of products contributes to increased business competitiveness such that if organizations do not continually change what they offer in products and services and how they create and deliver them to customers, they risk being overtaken by companies that do (Tidd & Bessant, 2009). Innovation has become a design imperative, where "knowledge" as a business resource is not "passively stored" or structured in fixed forms or static models, but at the ready to activate "technical-artistic" transformations of life (Thrift, 2006: 281). Active knowledge created by innovative design and design anthropologists is thus a way for firms to boost their difference from other organizations, as innovation becomes built into a continuous and inexhaustible process of emergence that goes beyond capital accumulation.

Third, new forms of designer-cum-consumer-led innovation help businesses not just compete in the global marketplace, but also solve trenchant environmental and social problems. Enhancing social well-being is led by new innovations often sourced from consumer–producer interactions. Consumers are expected to become more involved in acts of consumption itself, "through collecting, subscribing, experiencing and, in general, participating in all manner of collective acts of sense making" (Thrift, 2005: 7). In practices of "user-centered" innovation, organizations tap into consumer trends in commodity involvement and from user-based communities that thrive on branded products and services that make it easier for firms to follow product adaptations to customer needs and desires, and for them to flourish in the marketplace. As Eric von Hippel reports:

> User-centered innovation processes offer great advantages over the
> manufacturer-centric development systems that have been the mainstay of

commerce over hundreds of years. Users that innovate can develop exactly what they want, rather than rely on manufacturers to act as their (very often imperfect) agents. Moreover, users do not have to develop everything they need on their own: then can benefit from innovations developed and freely shared by others.

(2005: 1)

Firms are thus more likely to tap consumers for ideas (Starbucks rewards), and in return, reward consumers with both better basic service improvements and more expansive service innovation. For instance, Google challenges coders and hackers to infiltrate its software, which helps educate Google on how to improve its products. The adaptable (Miller, 1997) and the experimental (Thrift, 2006) modes of enterprise call for more innovative and interactive practices, encouraging open discourses from design anthropologists to make possible these new configurations of capitalism in the world.

In her compelling and thorough investigation of such personal, social, technological, and environmental changes, Miller draws together these and other configurations and adaptive changes over the years, and brings to light the myriad shifting relationship between anthropology and design. She further proposes alternative design and anthropological approaches which advocate an open and emergent ethnography that relocates the creative aspects of product, social, and human analysis into new collaborative spaces. Her important work offers fresh ways for considering the facets of innovation and practices of how a more thoughtful-designed form of anthropology can better engage the world of consumption, consumer intervention, corporate responsibility, and beyond.

References

Arnould, E. and C.J. Thompson. 2005. Consumer Culture Theory (CCT): Twenty Years of Research. *Journal of Consumer Research*, 31 (March), 868–882.

Baba, Marietta. L. 2006. Anthropology and Business. In H.J. Birx (Ed.), *Encyclopedia of Anthropology*. Thousand Oaks, CA: Sage Publications.

Boyd, D. and K. Crawford. 2011. Six Provocations for Big Data. Paper Presented at Oxford Internet Institute's Symposium on the Dynamics of the Internet and Society. http://ssrn.com/abstract=1926431.

Featherstone, M. 2007. *Consumer Culture and Postmodernism* (2nd Ed.). Los Angeles: Sage.

Horkheimer, Max and Theodor W. Adorno. (1944) 1969. *Dialectic of Enlightenment*. New York: Seabury Press.

Ingold, Tim. 2013. *Making: Anthropology, Archaeology, Art and Architecture*. New York: Routledge.

Ingold, Tim and Elizabeth Hallam. 2007. Creativity and Cultural Improvisation: An Introduction. In Elizabeth Hallam and Tim Ingold (Eds.), *Creativity and Cultural Improvisation*, 1–24. Oxford: Berg.

Klein, Naomi. 2000. *No logo: Taking Aim at the Brand Bullies*. New York: Picador.

Kotler, Philip and Gary Armstrong. 2016. *Principles of Marketing* (16th Ed.). Englewood Cliffs: Pearson.

Madsbjerg, C. and M. Rasmussen. 2014. *The Moment of Clarity*. Cambridge, MA: Harvard Business Press.

Malefyt, Timothy de Waal. 2017. Enchanting Technology, Guest Editorial. *Anthropology Today*, 33 (2), 1–2. (April).

Miller, Daniel. 1995. *Acknowledging Consumption*. London: Routledge.

———. 1997. *Capitalism—An Ethnographic Approach*. Oxford: Berg.

———. 2005. *Materialism, Politics, History and Culture*. Raleigh: Duke University Press.

Owen, Charles. 2006. Design Thinking: Notes on Its Nature and Use. *Design Research Quarterly*, 1 (12), 16–27.

Postrel, V. 2003. *The Substance of Style*. New York, NY: Harper Collins.

Sherry, John F., Jr. 2008. The Ethnographer's Apprentice: Trying Consumer Culture from the Outside In. *Journal of Business Ethics*, 80, 85–95.

Thrift, Nigel. 2005. *Knowing Capitalism*. London: Sage.

———. 2006. Re-Inventing Invention: New Tendencies in Capitalist Commodification. *Economy and Society*, 35, 2, 279–306.

Tidd, J. and J. Bessant. 2009. *Managing Innovation: Integrating Technological, Market, and Organizational Change*. Chichester, UK: John Wiley & Sons.

Von Hippel, Eric. 2005. *Democratizing Innovation*. Cambridge, MA: MIT Press.

PREFACE

The goal of this book is to contribute to the ongoing exploration and mapping of the transdisciplinary field of design anthropology, a field "in the making" that has emerged from a confluence of two distinct disciplines. Zoy Anastassakis and Barbara Szaniecki (2016) described this unique approach to practice and theory as having resulted from major shifts in both fields:

> Thus, while anthropology by means of ethnography is a descriptive prac-
> tice, anthropology by means of design is a practice of correspondence,
> which however, should not be limited to predicting as traditional designers
> do. To shift from predicting to correspondence, emphasis must go from
> the form itself to the process of conformation. In this perspective, design
> creativity does not lie in the novelty of the prefigured solutions, but in
> the ability of inhabitants of the world to respond to the changing circum-
> stances of life.
>
> *(2016: 124–125)*

Significant work has been done to identify the potential of and challenges to design anthropology. Members of the Network for Design Anthropology, a col-laborative venture between the Royal Danish Academy of Fine Arts, Aarhus University, and the University of Southern Denmark, have expanded their net-work of scholar-practitioners to explore themes that "rethink design in terms of time and futures" (Kjaersgaard et al., 2016: 5), and shift the anthropological gaze to include "ethnographies of the possible" (Halse, 2013: 182–183), imagined through collaborative experimentation, speculation, and improvisation.

Other contributions to design anthropology have come from diverse venues, including the EPIC network and conference, which has provided a platform for knowledge sharing among a diverse group of anthropologists, designers, and ethnographers who work in business, government, and not-for-profit organizations. The *Anthrodesign* Yahoo group, founded in 2002 by Natalie Hanson, is a practice-based sharing platform that has grown to nearly 3000 members (Hanson, 2017), and has provided a virtual space for meeting and exchange.

Writing this book has been a personal journey that has caused me to reconsider my own unorthodox academic and professional path. Having never neatly fit into a single disciplinary track, embracing design anthropology made perfect sense. The opportunity to work in collaboration with stakeholders to move beyond the traditional mode of observing, reporting, and prescribing solutions, to engage instead in facilitating collective future-making, is simultaneously exciting, empowering, and humbling.

Sometimes working on the level of people and their everyday lives seems outdated, overshadowed by current trends in Big Data, the hard data generated by statistical analytics and algorithmic logic that increasingly drives decision making. Yet we're reminded that "...it doesn't matter how much hard data we have in our hands. If we don't have a perspective on the human behavior involved, our insights have no power" (Madsjberg, 2017: x). The transdisciplinary melding of methods, theory, and practices from anthropology and design provides a *style of knowing* – the means of acquiring deep contextually grounded knowledge of human behavior – and *a way of making* that engages design creativity to respond to the ever-changing circumstances of our individual and collective lives.

Design anthropology continues to develop "as a cohesive field of its own... that both enhances and critically challenges its existing sources" (Murphy & Marcus, 2013: 251). The purpose of this book is to extend and open the conversation to engage existing, and attract new participants, so that community continues to happen.

References

Anastassakis, Z. and B. Szaniecki. 2016. Conversation Dispositifs: Towards a Transdisciplinary Design Anthropological Approach. In R.C. Smith, K.T. Vangkilde, M.G. Kjaersgaard, T. Otto, J. Halse, and T. Binder (Eds.), *Design Anthropological Futures*, 121–138. New York: Bloomsbury.

Hanson, N. 2017. Origins of Anthrodesign. Retrieved from https://nataliehanson.com/2017/01/09/origins-anthrodesign/.

Madsjberg, C. 2017. *Sensemaking: The Power of the Humanities in the Age of Algorithm.* New York: Hachette Books.

Murphy, K.M., & G.E. Marcus. 2013. Epilogue: Ethnography and Design, Ethnography in Design...Ethnography by Design. In W. Gunn, T. Otto, and R.C. Smith (Eds.), *Design Anthropology: Theory and Practice*, 251–267. New York: Bloomsbury.

ACKNOWLEDGMENTS

Behind every book is a network of supportive people who keep the author and the manuscript afloat, which is why, even though they are so personal, acknowledgments tend to be so similar. Without this cast of supportive actors "the book" would most likely never make it to press. Acknowledging the people, places, and things that provided the inspiration, motivation, and energy is an exercise in humility and gratitude.

First, thanks to Tim de Waal Malefyt for asking me to write this book. The prospect of capturing something in the process-of-becoming was both exciting and terrifying, usually more of the later. However, the challenge was irresistible. As contemporary disciplines, anthropology and design are continuing to evolve. There never was a merger of design and anthropology, nor was that ever the intention. Rather, the unique transdisciplinary field of design anthropology has emerged instead. Documenting the growth and development of this new approach has been an opportunity to study the diffusion of an innovation in research and praxis that continues to be recontextualized.

I also want to thank Ken Riopelle for collaborating to identify and analyze the dynamic social networks that are giving structure and substance to design anthropology. Ken's expertise with the tools of dynamic social network analysis allowed us to craft a story about the ongoing diffusion of design anthropology as an innovation and its prospects for being recognized as a new transdisciplinary field.

This book would not have been written without constant encouragement and interest from many other individuals. Although they weren't exactly sure what this thing was that I was writing about, the excited anticipation of friends, family, former students, and colleagues kept the project going. Special thanks to Dagmar Lorenz for her friendship and many chats over dinners during which she shared her experience as an author and helped me come to believe in the process. And beyond 'thank you,' to my beautiful daughter, Jessica Knapp-Cruz, and my husband and life partner, David A. Miller, who tirelessly read and reread, worked on graphics and indexing, offered suggestions, and generally kept me afloat. Much love – you are both amazing.

Christine Miller
Chicago, Illinois
April 2017

INTRODUCTION

Granted that disorder spoils pattern; it also provides the materials of pattern. Order implies restriction; from all possible materials, a limited selection has been made and from all possible relations a limited set has been used. So disorder by implication is unlimited, no pattern has been realised in it, but its potential for patterning is indefinite. This is why, though we seek to create order, we do not simply condemn disorder. We recognise that it is destructive to existing patterns; also that it has potentiality. It symbolises both danger and power.

(Douglas, 2002: 117)

Chaos, Purity, and Danger

In a world where the ground seems to be shifting under our feet, it is easy to accept the trend to "challenge boundaries," and specifically, to challenge disciplinary boundaries. After all, disciplines are a phenomenon of our social worlds; they do not exist in the natural world. Devised to stake out a field of professional expertise and practice, disciplines are "social constructions," collectively created understandings about meaning and significance that are shared within social groups (Berger & Luckmann, 1967). In many fields, the silos of disciplinary practice have begun to give way to creating permeable boundaries that allow for cross-disciplinary encounters where specialty areas emerge and develop, for example, biochemical engineering or business and design anthropology. The dissolution of once clearly defined disciplinary boundaries has resulted in the need to explain these seemingly unlikely hybrids. It is the new exotic: strange, unorthodox, and even somehow wonderful.

The resulting hybrid fields present a challenge to how we identify and introduce ourselves. Within professional settings this is situationally and contextually specific. If I am with anthropologists, I am likely to identify myself as a business or design anthropologist. If I am with a group of designers, then I introduce myself as an anthropologist. And if I am with business professionals, I might also introduce myself as an anthropologist. If I decide to introduce myself as a design anthropologist, things become confusing very quickly. Within anthropology circles this would draw a mixed reception. Designers might be more willing to accept this identity, but be very suspicious as to whether I am *really* a designer. Business people would probably be at a complete loss since they would wonder what an *anthropologist* was doing there in the first place. But a design anthropologist? Not likely. It is too far-fetched, at least in the United States where design anthropology as such is not well known within the business and commercial world or even for that matter, within anthropology.

I am not advocating for a return to the familiar comfort of strict disciplinary boundaries, nor am I launching a call to action to "circle the wagons"[1] to fend off potential border crossers that (mis)appropriate concepts and methods. That the disorder creates chaos is not newsworthy. My intention is to provide the background – to recount a version of the story – of why and how the field of design anthropology has come to be, what it is today, and the trajectories it might take in the future. To do this requires that I first address some basic questions. What is design anthropology? How was this integration of anthropological inquiry and design practice able to occur, especially in the ways that it has in particular contexts? Why do practitioners and scholars of design anthropology self-identify as such? What does it mean to be a design anthropologist? How do design anthropologists explain to other practitioners and scholars within and external to their field, to themselves, and to the general public, why this practice is meaningful, significant, and necessary? Furthermore, how do they communicate and demonstrate the unique value of their contribution to teammates and clients? This is where the story begins.

What This Book Is About

This book is about the transdisciplinary field of design anthropology, the global forces and conditions that facilitated its emergence, the people that have contributed to its emergence, and those who are likely to shape its future. It is also about the evolution of two disciplines, design and anthropology, and their convergence within commercial, social, and organizational arenas. It is about the invention and diffusion of new practices, the recontextualization of ethnographic inquiry within design, the comingling of anthropological and design research and practice, and movement towards a transformative, interventionist anthropology. It is about how encounters between anthropology and "designerly ways of knowing" (Cross, 2006), thinking, and doing have impacted the evolution of both disciplines. Finally, it is about the movement to formalize the nascent field of design anthropology, and about how the relationship between the two fields might develop in the future given the dynamic global forces that continue to impact them both.

The aim of this book is to go beyond describing the outcomes of "ethnographically-informed design" (Blomberg & Burrell, 2009) that characterized early encounters between anthropologists and designers, to an exploration of current praxis that is moving anthropologists from their traditional roles as participant observers, advocates, and critics. Vignettes that illustrate how the integration of anthropological inquiry with design principles and practices have evolved over time make clear that a new and distinctly different "style of knowing" (Otto & Smith, 2013) is emerging. In part, the book provides an exploration of practices and *praxis*[2] that describe this work: the perspectives and frameworks employed in approaching problems, and the methods used by design anthropologists to collect, analyze, and synthesize findings that create opportunities for intervention and transformation in the everyday lives of people, in their relations with each other, and to the planet.

Much has been written to document the developments within anthropology that led to the migration of anthropological praxis to organizational and commercial arenas (for example, see Robinson, 1994; Wasson, 2000; Blomberg & Burrell, 2009; Cefkin, 2009; Suchman, 2011). However, relatively little attention within the United States context has been directed toward the emergence of design anthropology as a "distinct style of knowing" (Otto & Smith, 2013: 10), learning, and doing, resulting from integrating anthropological inquiry and design practices, and from transdisciplinary collaboration between designers and anthropologists. Due to the collaborative efforts of a growing network of anthropologists, designers, and ethnographers, design anthropology is being recognized as an emerging field which embodies a unique and distinctive form of ethnographic inquiry and cultural analysis that is motivated by an intentionally interventionist and transformative perspective. Although these collaborative networks exist around the world, several major centers of practice, teaching, and scholarship can be identified that have explicitly set out to define and articulate the field.[3] The field as such is "young" (Otto & Smith, 2013: 11). The number of practitioners and scholars in the United States who explicitly identify as design anthropologists is relatively small, but increasing. Their work is often considered a subset of business anthropology, although the field is explicitly transdisciplinary. In the United States, recognition of the field in its own right, as *a distinct style of knowing* that is defined by new practices, methods, and a growing body of literature, has yet to reach the level that exists in other parts of the world, especially in Europe.

With this in mind, the purpose in writing this book is to further the diffusion and articulation of design anthropology as a distinctive field of inquiry and knowledge production that represents an evolving trajectory within the social sciences and, in particular, within anthropology. My intention is to pick up the threads of previous contributions to contemporary ethnographic inquiry, building on the growing body of literature that furthers our understanding of cultural analysis in the contexts of social, commercial and organizational settings. There are many threads that make up what we call design anthropology. The goal here is to continue to bring them together in a meaningful and cohesive way.

As a contribution to previous and current efforts, the book has three aims: first, to explore from a primarily United States vantage point, the forces and conditions that shaped the evolution of design and anthropology, making their encounter in commercial, organizational, and institutional realms probable if not inevitable. Second, it aims to trace the emergence of design anthropology as a unique form of praxis. Finally, it seeks to contribute to a vision for design anthropology as a global *community of practice* comprised of unique localized *collaborative innovation networks*.

Who This Book Is For

This book is written with a broad audience in mind. While it is intended to engage in ongoing conversations between anthropologists, designers, and design anthropologists, it also aims to appeal to practitioners from diverse fields who want to understand what design anthropology is about, why anthropologists are increasingly visible in contemporary settings outside academia, and why many companies are embracing design beyond form and aesthetics. The book will be helpful to members of corporations and organizations that deploy – or want to deploy- pluridisciplinary[4] teams that include anthropologists, designers, engineers, marketers, and other business disciplines. It aims to introduce anthropologists to the design process and designers to ethnographic practice, the thick description that is anthropology's signature methodology. Finally, it seeks to speak to students of both anthropology and design who are questioning how rapidly changing conditions might impact the direction of their fields, and the opportunities available to them in their careers.

Serendipitously, I am writing at a time when some designers and anthropologists have called for a "time out" from their 25-plus-year relationship. It is interesting to be writing about design anthropology when each discipline is stepping back to regroup and assess the costs and benefits of their intense cross-disciplinary collaboration. During the relatively short encounter between design and anthropology, much of what has been developed is the result of ongoing experimentation and invention. Methods are often improvised in the moment by simultaneously reaching back and looking forward to construct frameworks of sense making in the continually unfolding present. Theory emerges from practice.

Reflecting on the relationship between design and anthropology as it has evolved over the years, Murphy and Marcus noted that although it has been "asymmetrical, with anthropology almost exclusively subordinated to the needs of design" (2013: 252), the imbalance has been useful in deciphering the similarities or "correspondences" and the dissimilarities between the two disciplines including their unique processes, temporal orientation (Otto & Smith, 2013: 17–18), tools, and attitudes toward success. The time seems right for evaluating the costs and benefits of the relationship as part of a broader assessment of anthropology in light of the role and production of ethnography as its *signature methodology* in contemporary fieldwork. My aspiration for this book is that it continues the conversation within practice and within the academy, taking inventory of the great, the good, and the not-so-good aspects of this close disciplinary encounter. It is important to remember that the encounter between these two unique knowledge traditions has a relatively short history, and that it is, for the most part, a collaborative experiment. Achieving transdisciplinary collaboration is a tedious process of experimentation that includes wrong turns and outright failures as well as scattered successes which over time form a pattern that begins to define a unique practice. Disciplinary taboos, such as shifting the focus of anthropological description to intervention, are violated. Yet the urgency to remain relevant and responsive in the complexity of an increasingly connected and networked world provides the impetus and motivation to continue to invent, and to experiment, test, and validate.

Consequently, efforts continue to formalize design anthropology as a cohesive field of its own "that both enhances and critically challenges its original sources." (Gunn et al, 2013: 251) The purpose of this book is to extend and open the conversation to engage existing and attract new participants so that community continues to happen.

Structure of the Book

This book is organized in five chapters. Chapters 1 and 2 explore the confluence of anthropology and design through the lens of history, tracing the origins of design anthropology through its roots in both fields. Chapter 3 proposes eight emerging principles that are applied to operationalize design anthropological practice. Chapter 4 looks into the communities and networks that comprise design anthropology, and the individuals who are influential in bringing the disciplines together through client projects, by supporting colleagues and friends in launching initiatives and start-ups, by creating forums for sharing and exchanging information, and by developing academic programs that introduce students to design anthropological practice and theory. By applying social network analysis, Chapter 4 presents a glimpse of current and possible trajectories for design anthropology. Exploring these trajectories in collaboration with network analyst Ken Riopelle, we were able to identify and analyze the social networks that are drivers of change, and to speculate on the possibilities for future developments in the field. Recognizing that "the future of all ethnographic inquiry will unfold through the work of its practitioners" (Murphy & Marcus, 2013: 265), this section surveys the landscape of centers of learning and doing, focusing on the continuing importance of key individuals, networks, forums, and core contributors, and the role of institutions in the education and training of future design anthropologists.

Chapter 5 concludes with observations that are intended to encourage further discussion. From the vantage point of the present, we are able to identify emerging practitioners and centers of practice, teaching, and learning, both in traditional institutions and in the commercial arena. The challenge of capturing the dynamics of an emerging field is daunting. "Getting it right" when there are so many voices, forums, and organizations involved is a matter of jumping onto a moving train where the destination is up to the passengers and is yet to be decided. Welcome aboard!

Notes

1 The phrase "circle the wagons" refers to the practice on the North American frontier when wagon trains were under attack. The Conestoga or "covered" wagons were drawn into a circle to provide shelter from hostile advances, and to protect people and property. Here the phrase suggests a response to a perceived incursion or attack on the purity of a disciplinary field.
2 *Praxis* is a Latin term used to describe the process of how theory and practice inform each other, or how skills and knowledge are enacted and embodied in practice.
3 Emerging centers of activity include the Center for Ethnography at the University of California, Irvine; Swinburne University of Technology, Victoria, Australia; IIT Institute of Design in Chicago; and the University of North Texas, Denton. The Research Network for Design Anthropology is a collaboration between The Royal Danish Academy of Fine Arts, Aarhus University, and the University of Southern Denmark, funded for 2 years by the Danish Research Council (https://kadk.dk/en/center-codesign-research/research-network-design-anthropology).
4 In characterizing teams, I use the term "pluridisciplinary" to emphasize the qualitative differences between multidisciplinary, interdisciplinary, and transdisciplinary teams. While all three forms are made up of members from more than one discipline, pluridisciplinary is used when the nature of the team is unknown (Choi & Pak, 2006).

References

Berger, Peter L. and Thomas Luckmann. 1967. *The Social Construction of Reality: A Treatise in the Sociology of Knowledge.* New York: Anchor Books.

Blomberg, Jeanette and Mark Burrell. 2009. An Ethnographic Approach to Design. In A. Sears and J.A. Jacko (Eds.), *Human-Computer Interaction: Development Process*, 71–93. Boca Raton, FL: CRC Press.

Cefkin, Melissa (Ed.). 2009. *Ethnography and the Corporate Encounter: Reflections on Research in and of Corporations.* New York: Berghahn Books.

Choi, Bernard C.K. and Anita W.P. Pak. 2006. Multidisciplinary, Interdisciplinary and Transdisciplinary in Health Research, Services, Education and Policy: 1. Definitions, Objectives, and Evidence of Effectiveness. *Clinical and Investigative Medicine*, 29(6), 351–364.

Cross, Nigel. 2006. *Designerly Ways of Knowing.* London: Springer-Verlag.

Douglas, Mary. 2002. *Purity and Danger: An Analysis of Concepts of Pollution and Taboo.* New York: Routledge.

Gunn, Wendy, Ton Otto, and Rachel C. Smith (Eds.). 2013. *Design Anthropology: Theory and Practice.* New York: Bloomsbury.

Murphy, Kevin and George E. Marcus. 2013. Epilogue: Ethnography and Design, Ethnography in Design…Ethnography by Design. In W. Gunn, T. Otto, and R.C. Smith (Eds.), *Design Anthropology: Theory and Practice*, 251–267. New York: Bloomsbury.

Otto, Ton and Rachel C. Smith. 2013. Design Anthropology: A Distinct Style of Knowing. In W. Gunn, T. Otto, and R.C. Smith (Eds.), *Design Anthropology: Theory and Practice*, 1–31. New York: Bloomsbury.

Robinson, Rick E. 1994. Making Sense of Making Sense: Frameworks and Organizational Perception. *Design Management Journal*, 5, 8–15.

Suchman, Lucy A. 2011. Anthropological Relocations and the Limits of Design. *Annual Review of Anthropology*, 40, 1–18.

Wasson, Christina. 2000. Ethnography in the Field of Design. *Human Organization*, 59(4), 377–388.

1

MAKING THE STRANGE FAMILIAR
AND THE FAMILIAR STRANGE

Introduction

The goal of this chapter is to retrace the evolution of the anthropological discipline in the aftermath of two World Wars and the opening decades of the new millennium, focusing on the people, events, and debates that provide a backdrop for a current discussion of design anthropology and its genesis. Although it is not possible to include all the people, places, events, journal articles, books, conferences, and debates that transpired to shape anthropology during this tumultuous period, the aim is to highlight events that signaled major paradigm shifts and reveal how and why design anthropology came to be what it is *today*. "Today" is a word that came up repeatedly in conducting the research for this book. For the purpose of this chapter, today is understood as "the present," which Tobias Rees (2008b) defined as "a historical, open moment in which what is or what has been is, at least potentially, changing." Thus, the objective of this chapter is to capture what Rabinow et al. refer to as the *residual, dominant,* and the *emergent,* the three categories that constitute the present state of anthropology as a dynamic phenomenon (2008: 95).

The sections in this chapter describe the trajectories of anthropology over time that created the possibility for an encounter between anthropology and design, and the eventual emergence of the transdisciplinary field of design anthropology. As they facilitated this occurrence, the history and debates of the recent past and the present prefigure the emergence of new subfields such as business and design anthropology. They provide a context for anthropology's positioning in relation to design and design-driven innovation as well as the prospects of an anthropology of design (Suchman, 2011).

Design anthropology is an emerging transdisciplinary field characterized by an approach that integrates anthropological methods, theory, frameworks and critique with design principles and practices to address an increasingly wide range of complex systems-level problems facing contemporary societies, institutions, and organizations. Design anthropology extends beyond the boundaries of both anthropology and design to include practitioner-scholars from a wide range of disciplines that work within commercial, organizational, and academic contexts using descriptive and generative research tools (Gunn, 2008; Kilbourn, 2013), common theoretical and methodological approaches, and shared work practices. It draws from many intellectual traditions, philosophies, and disciplines. However, at its core, design anthropology incorporates tenets that root it within two primary fields: design and anthropology. An evolving set of principles includes a commitment to participatory design and a focus on collective engagements (e.g., Halse's "design events") as *singular events* that open new potentialities for creating not-yet existing social realities (Kapferer, 2010), an interventionist and transformative approach to anthropological practice that interweaves past and present to imagine possible futures (Halse, 2013), design principles and creative practices, reflexivity and critique, and an evolving ethical code that seeks to decolonize current trends in design innovation (Tunstall, 2013). These principles have evolved through the series of developments and experiments in two distinct fields, anthropology and design, to emerge as a distinctive form of transdisciplinary praxis that moves research into action.

The Anthropological Roots of Design Anthropology

Anthropology has always been a dynamic field and work in progress. Over its 100 plus year history, it has been rife with debates resulting from diverse approaches to the study of human beings, their societies, and cultures. The purpose of the following sections is to bring together many threads that provided a foundation for design anthropology to emerge not only as a unique expression of anthropology's ongoing evolution, but also as the response of two distinct fields of inquiry that share a common affinity. Beyond tracing design anthropology's connection to legacy anthropology and anthropologists, as well as to contemporary debates about encounters between anthropology and design-driven innovation, this exploration brings to light the conversations and forces that are influencing the course of design anthropology as another in a series of evolving forms of anthropological inquiry, a "distinctive style of knowing" that builds on an increasing body of practice-based theory.

The focus in examining the anthropological roots of design anthropology necessarily extends beyond the United States context. Equally important sites of design anthropological knowledge production exist, especially in Europe, which are shaping the field in somewhat different but arguably more significant ways. The intention is not to privilege one site over another, but rather to illustrate how prevailing conditions and developments in local contexts resulted in various manifestations of design anthropology that stress different aspects of practice.

Tracing the Threads

A growing body of literature documents the work of anthropologists and ethnographers in commercial and institutional settings as they engaged in corporate ethnography, studies of Human–Computer Interaction (HCI), user-centered research, and in collaboration on pluridisciplinary teams in commerical ventures with the aim to "...provide a perspective on the relations between humans and the artifacts that they design and use" (Blomberg & Burrell, 2009: 72). Other texts describe the early encounters between anthropologists and designers and the adaptation of ethnography by designers. Christina Wasson's article, "Ethnogrphy in the Field of Design" (2000), provides an overview of the extension of applied anthropology to design, tracing how ethnography was adopted and adapted by design firms. Taking a critical perspective, Wasson raised concerns about the lack of depth in "design ethnography" citing examples such as the AEIOU framework, a method developed at E-Lab that was used to help interpret video footage, observations, code data, and develop models to address clients' issues (2000: 382). Wasson notes that the framework initially suffered from limitations that included identifying broad cultural patterns and ignored "questions of change, history and political economy" (2000: 385). Wasson mentions that the ongoing iteration of that particular framework brought improvement. Once the initial experiments in applying "ethnography" in user-centered design were reported by the media, many design firms began to offer some form of "ethnographic research," often an overly simplistic (and typically incorrect) facsimile that was conducted by untrained staff.

Although it appears obvious from this point in time, a recontextualized "ethnographic" practice in design is not commensurate with ethnography in the antrhopological sense, first, because the meaning of ethnography is not the same (Ingold, 2014).[1] Second, the end goals of each discipline have traditionally been very different. Ethical allegiance is not the same: anthropologists have struggled to reconcile the legacy of their affiliation with colonial powers by strengthening their ethical allegiance to the subjects of their studies. Although this is changing, designers have traditionally focused on ethics that priviledge and protect their client's data. The appropriation of "ethnography" by designers and other practitioners has resulted in heated debates among anthropologists and within the academy. Beyond a question of the quality of research, there were well-founded concerns about ethics, attitudes toward study subjects, and transparency of study results that led to a revision of the American Anthropological Association's Statement on Ethics in 2012 (Miller, 2017). As rapid technological advances have ushered in new forms of data collection through the use of sensors (Business Wire, 2012) and ubiquitous video survelliance, ethical concerns will continue to be a hotly debated issue within anthropology.

Anthropology and Business

In her essay on *Anthropology and Business*, Marietta Baba (2006) described a new form of interdisciplinary practice as "ethnographically informed design of products, services, and systems" "resting on the notion of a marriage between ethnography and design" (2006: 108), which she attributed to the collaboration between anthropologist Lucy Suchman and Rick Robinson, founder of several design firms including E-Lab and more recently IOTA. Baba draws a link to the forces of industrialization, tracing the roots of the new interdisciplinary subfield, which she notes was also referred to as *design ethnography*, back to the efforts of Fredrick Taylor and Elton Mayo to "improve interactions between people and equipment in the production process." These early efforts to study "the human factor in production" evolved to become the field of *human factors*, a multiple disciplinary specialty that incorporates ergonomic and psychological aspects into the design process. Human factors remain to this day a fundamental component of industrial design practice.

Prior to Baba's essay, Ann Jordan's *Business Anthropology* (Jordan, 2003) provided a primer for practitioners and students of anthropology. Jordan explained that she does not apply her skills in working "with farmers in Rajasthan or the Sherpas near Mount Everest" (2003: 1), but rather in multinational corporations. Touching on a range of themes, she includes a chapter entitled "Design Anthropology" in which she writes that "Ethnographic techniques have become popular in the design field because they fill a void in the research data" (2003: 76). She notes designers' dependence on human factors research that developed from cognitive psychology and marketing research.

> While human factors research is useful for understanding the best way to design some products, for others, it is too abstract and removed from everyday reality because it is often conducted in controlled environments, like labs (Van Veggel n.d.). In addition, this type of research focuses on what goes on in individuals' heads and does not take into account the social and cultural context and group interaction. Thus, there is no opportunity to observe and learn from the rich interaction of social beings in which products are not only used but also understood.
>
> *(2003: 77)*

Citing multiple sources, Cefkin (2010: 10–13) provides an overview of the "disciplinary contexts" of ethnography in and of corporations noting the earliest encounters, anthropological studies of the workplace dating back to the Hawthorne Studies (Mayo, 1945; Schwartzman, 1993) conducted between 1924–1932. Cefkin and other authors have noted the influence of Scandinavian workplace ethnography and trade union projects from the 1970s and 1980s that introduced cooperative and participatory design, now recognized as fundamental principles of design anthropology (Cefkin, 2010; Otto & Smith, 2013; Tunstall, 2013).

Business and industrial anthropology's anthropological roots have been well-documented chronologically, and from the perspective of intellectual and conceptual contributions. As design anthropology is becoming articulated as a unique field in its own right, an interdisciplinary body of literature is emerging. However, other aspects of anthropology that account for design anthropology's distinctive characteristics have, until recently, received less attention. I refer here to insights of legacy and contemporary anthropologists that foreshadow and resonate with the evolving tenets of design anthropology. These threads – observations, insights, and conversations – emerge, are forgotten, and then reappear at other points in time. Bringing them to light not only confirms the ties to anthropology, but also suggests how a deeper investigation of these ties can provide potential directions in which design anthropology *as a distinct style of knowing* might unfold.

The following sections revolve around three related and reoccurring themes that have dominated anthropology in the last half of the twentieth century and continue to be discussed in somewhat different guises today. Although they appear in many complex forms, the themes can be summarized as, first, calls to reinvent anthropology by moving beyond its association with the colonialist past; second, debates as to what a "reinvented" anthropology might be; and finally, how a reinvented "anthropology of the contemporary" would remain true to its roots. Collectively, these themes provide a framework for the remaining sections of this chapter. Each theme has been extensively and authoritatively documented in anthropological literature, primarily in texts that are not likely to be accessed by anyone outside the discipline. Yet if anthropology is to have a stake as an equal partner with design in this emerging field, which some have argued it should but often does not have (Wasson, 2000; Suchman, 2011), its unique value will need to be articulated and demonstrated. The sections that follow draw on several sources to reveal the past as a deeply meaningful source of anthropology's current and potential value as a contemporary field, as well as its transformative relocation and integration within design anthropology.

"Anthropology: Its Achievements and Future"

By 1966, the calls for "reinventing anthropology" were already well-established and documented.[2] Two decades before *Writing Culture* was published, Claude Lévi-Strauss predicted that, "Anthropology will survive in a changing world by allowing itself to perish in order to be born again under a new guise" (1966: 126).[3] Lévi-Strauss made a plea in this essay for the crucial importance of continuing to study rapidly disappearing indigenous human societies. The language Lévi-Strauss used to describe the subjects of existing ethnographic studies reflects the rhetorical conventions of the day. The sentiments and attitudes toward subjects, the conditions he describes, the problems that anthropologists were attempting to address, and *why* the discipline existed – its *reason d'etre* – are different from what most anthropologists experience and know anthropology to be today.

Fifty years after its publication, we are likely to be sobered[4] by what he describes as the "high rate of extinction afflicting primitive tribes all over the world." Although we are aware of their demise in a historical sense, Lévi-Strauss went on to provide a comparison of numbers of human populations at the beginning of the nineteenth century to the figures that survived into the 1960s. He notes that most if not all that survived were "hungry and disease ridden, threatened in their deserts by mining plants, atom bomb test grounds, and missile ranges." That these human populations, for the most part, crossed over to extinction did nothing to stop the ongoing processes of industrial capitalist expansion. Today we can add climate change to Lévi-Strauss' list. That the topic of extinct human populations rates so little of the world's attention is due in part to the fact that so very few of these people remain. Those who do are effectively rendered invisible: either they exist as hidden or "problem" populations within contemporary society, or they are so physically and/or psychologically marginalized as to be irrelevant to much of the contemporary world. While we campaign against the extinction of other species, we do not often or readily realize that our own species is and has long been equally in peril.

In this short essay, Lévi-Strauss opens with a memory of his time in the United States. He had come across a bookstore that was selling secondhand volumes of the *Annual Report of the Bureau of American Ethnology* which existed from 1879 until it merged in 1965 with the Smithsonian's Department of Anthropology to form the Smithsonian Office of Anthropology.[5] In spite of what he noted was for him at the time a significant investment,[6] he eventually purchased all of the available volumes "at the cost of some privations." He was enthralled with the volumes which provided him with a window to an "irredeemable past," where "the civilization of the American Indian had suddenly come alive through the physical contact that these contemporary books established between me and their time" (1966: 124).

By opening a window to anthropology as he and his contemporaries knew and lived it, Lévi-Strauss did something similar for me. I could "hear" and feel his grief for the human cultures that were slipping away, as well as for the human beings that were members of those societies. Yet in reading his words, there was still a sense of detachment that was not unknown in his time, an attitude that comes from being the outside observer: one who maintains an analytical distance, one who can walk away. For those among whom the studies took place, the losses were not only material, but also symbolic.

After reading this essay, I experienced what Paul Rabinow wrote in describing Richard McKeon's[7] ability "to cite both Ockham and Heidegger and show they illuminated current issues while in other ways being simply discordant from each other and the present" (Rabinow et al., 2008: 20). In spite of the "datedness" that is obvious in a reading today, there is much in this essay that is not only poignant, but also relevant and meaningful historically, methodologically, and theoretically. For example, at one point Lévi-Strauss explains how problems that had been neglected – the elasticity of crop yields, and the relationship between yield and the amount of work involved – could provide keys to deciphering the significance of established knowledge, such as the social and religious importance of yams throughout Micronesia. The apparatus that facilitated discoveries which constituted anthropological knowledge production and expertise was wrapped into the *technical considerations,* or "what counts as data" (Rabinow et al., 2008: 16–17) in the discipline: the methods through which data was collected, as well as the kinds of data that were selected for collection. This is another aspect of the technological changes that are currently impacting ethnographic practice aside from the ethical concerns that were mentioned previously.

Lévi-Strauss argued that new life could be given to time-worn questions that continue to be relevant in the contemporary world. For example,

> an exhausted question – the origin of the potter's wheel – by pointing out that an invention is neither simply a new mechanical device, nor a material object that can be described objectively, but rather a manner of proceeding which may avail itself of a number of different devices, some crude and others more elaborate.
>
> *(1966: 127)*

Our contemporary preoccupation with invention and innovation can benefit from insights like this one.[8]

Lévi-Strauss mentioned Sir John Fraser's 1908 inaugural lecture at Liverpool University in which Fraser stated that "classical anthropology was at its end." Developments over subsequent years – two World Wars and technological, commercial, and industrial advances that contributed to the demise of those societies that were already at risk – Levi-Strauss argues that "however disastrous," there were developments to cheer (1966: 125). At one point he noted that,

> It has become the fashion in certain circles to speak of anthropology as a science on the wane, on account of the rapid disappearance of its traditional subject matter: the so-called primitives. Or else it is claimed that in order to survive, anthropology should abandon fundamental research and become an applied science, dealing with the problems of developing countries and the pathological aspects of our own society.
>
> *(1966: 125)*

Stating that he did not discourage these new research directions or think them uninteresting, Lévi-Strauss maintained that it was precisely because they were "becoming extinct" that the study of "so-called primitive peoples" should remain a priority. He acknowledged (and condoned) that the field was evolving, exploring new problems that had so far received little attention. This, he explained, should be reassuring as far as anthropology's future: anthropology's perspective, its methods, and its value would endure. And yet he wondered, "When the last native culture will have disappeared from the Earth and our only interlocutor will be the electronic computer, it will have become so remote that we may well doubt whether the same kind of approach will deserve to be called 'anthropology' any longer" (1966: 127). Lévi-Strauss might not have been able to envision anthropology extended to the contemporary.

If there is any doubt as to the extent to which anthropology has changed over the nearly 50 years since its publication, reading this essay puts them to rest. One might imagine how anthropologists in Lévi-Strauss' day would react to the current paradigm of active engagement with "study subjects" and interventions involving "users" in participatory design aimed at transforming existing conditions. What would Malinowski say if it were suggested that he extend the frame-breaking methodology of participant observation to include the *participant facilitator* or Kilbourn's *facilitating provoker* (2013: 17)? How would one introduce a collective problem-solving orientation like those that are espoused and widely practiced by design anthropologists today? In keeping with the goal of attending to the *residual, dominant,* and the *emergent,* acknowledging the categories that constitute a dynamic phenomenon, like the present state of anthropology, means revisiting the anthropological archives to be reminded of the dramatic shifts that have occurred within the discipline. Equally important, we must preserve the insights that can both inform contemporary practice and sharpen our critique of it.

Making the Strange Familiar and the Familiar Strange

"Making the strange familiar and the familiar strange" is not only the legacy of anthropology, but also its present and very likely will be, in some form, its future. Anthropology holds that within whatever "strange" is or was, there are familiar elements that reflect our own stories, conditions, and times. This process of sense-making goes to the core of the unique art, craft, and science of anthropological knowledge production. Making the familiar strange reflects the relatively recent turn in the field from its focus on the "faraway other" to the shifting of the anthropological gaze to the study of present time and societies; in other words, what Paul Rabinow, George Marcus, and others (Rabinow et al., 2008) refer to as "the contemporary."

The emergence of new forms of practice and inquiry, new problems, and "relocations" of contemporary anthropology does not negate the persistent need to carry on with *all* of anthropology's agendas, those that Lévi-Strauss maintained were "more urgent and more important" (1966: 127). Anthropology as a discipline and community of practice has demonstrated that it is big enough to accommodate many research agendas. But it will do so, as it has done from its inception, in the spirit of critical self-analysis.

The Way We Were: The Legacy of the 1960s through the 1980s

In the wake of World War II, calls to "reinvent" anthropology intensified. The shifts that moved the discipline from its traditional focus on ethnographic description of "the faraway other" had been noted by many authors. For example, echoing sentiments in the final years of the 1960s, Dell Hymes asks in her introduction to *Reinventing Anthropology*, "If anthropology did not exist, would it have to be invented? If it were to be reinvented, would it be the anthropology we have now? To both questions, the answer, I think, is no" (1974: 3).

Hymes correctly predicted that the discipline is not what it was in the 1960s. Although terms like "reinvention" and "renewal" were widely used, what they meant, precisely, was unclear. Anthropology, specifically sociocultural anthropology, has shifted in many ways from its traditional projects. Intense ongoing intradisciplinary debates continue over a variety of concerns about the relocation of anthropology to commercial and corporate arenas, and within the public sector and military. At the same time, new forms of anthropological engagement that explicitly entail intervention and transformative forms of practice are giving rise to new sets of questions, problems, and concerns about the role of anthropology, and the positioning of anthropologists in the contemporary world.

Paradigm shifts result in ruptures and fissures that challenge the survival of a discipline. Such is the case for anthropology. How could the legacy of the past be reconciled to the realities of the present? And what did that mean for the future? Calling out that which did not serve to ensure relevance or survival of the discipline was an arduous and painful process. Had it not occurred, anthropology would likely have lost relevance in the contemporary world as it was inextricably bound to its studies of the "primitive," the premodern, and the past.

Designs for an Anthropology of the Contemporary

In the "Introduction" (2008b) to *Designs for an Anthropology of the Contemporary*, Tobias Rees describes his experience as an anthropology and philosophy student in the mid-1990s at the University of Tübingen.[9] His education was based on the history of ethnography "organized in the form of paradigmatic works in their chronological succession."

> The story we encountered was – on the level of concepts and methods – full of ruptures. And yet it was – around the level of the theme around which it evolved – a most coherent one: anthropology was the science of the far away other, the "premodern," the "primitive."
>
> *(Rees, 2008b: 1)*

The culmination of his study included a critique of anthropology's role in colonialism, a review of the emergence of multiple voices in ethnographic accounts, and a reading of *Writing Culture: The Poetics and Politics of Ethnography* (Clifford & Marcus, 1986). As Rees explained,

> The volume introduced an irreversible fracture between (a part of) the older generation, which defended the classical anthropology project, and (a part of) the younger one, which found itself compelled to move beyond

what appeared to them as a repertoire of well-tried concepts, to find new ways of practicing anthropology, new ways of producing anthropological knowledge…

(2008b: 5)

Writing Culture left Rees with a sense that it brought the history of anthropology to an end,

It seemed to do so, epistemologically speaking, in showing that the pre-modern was less found than constructed (by the rhetorical conventions of a particular genre of writing, *ethnography*), and so it put the whole undertaking of anthropology, its methods, its concepts, and even its object, radically in question.

(2008b: 2)

What could come after? In retrospect, rather than an "end," *Writing Culture* marked another in a series of fissures and shifts within anthropology. In fact, a turn was well underway, ignited by what Rees identified as three developments that continued anthropology's self-examination and critique: the rise of a new post–World War II sensitivity, the emergence of a new anthropological paradigm represented by Clifford Geertz's program of interpretive anthropology, and the availability of new anthropological tools (2008b: 3).

These developments illuminate conditions that contributed to anthropology's ongoing process of internal self-critique and reevaluation, turning up the volume on two fundamental questions: *What are we doing and why are we doing it?* The critique of ethnography in *Writing Culture* amplified the call to continue a major inventory of the discipline, taking stock of its legacy to determine what had value, what might be repurposed, and the attitudes and perspectives that would need to be overhauled or weeded out.

Despite its relatively short length, *Designs* is a work of major importance that requires special attention. The following section highlights topics within the dialogues that address the major shifts and turns within anthropology over the tumultuous period covering the final decades of the twentieth century to the first decade of the twenty-first century.

Looking Back to Move Forward

The series of dialogues that cover the struggles to free anthropology from the stereotypes, romanticism, and colonial era baggage of its past, as well as efforts to preserve its legacy, are documented in what became *Designs for an Anthropology of the Contemporary* (Rabinow et al., 2008). Through the personal perspectives of the dialogue partners, *Designs* provides a graduate-level refresher course on anthropological history and theory in the last half of the twentieth century. On one hand, tensions within the academy and among colleagues were rampant as debates raged on regarding what should be preserved, what should be repurposed, and what needed to be relegated to anthropology's dark days in service to colonialism. On the other hand, a multitude of projects were launched that opened the way for areas of interdisciplinary inquiry, new forms of conceptualizing the realities of the contemporary world, new topics, perspectives, practices, and experimentation.

Recounting his position in the middle of one of these less hostile debates, Rees relates how, while a graduate student at Berkeley in 2002, Rabinow sent him Marcus' reaction to his soon-to-be-published book, *Anthropos Today* (Rabinow, 2003). The series of conversations that ensued were described by Rees as a presentation of "thinking in motion" and "a conversation across generations" (2008a: 115). The conversations span the broad and tumultuous swath of anthropology's history from the 1960s through the 1980s, which was captured in *Designs for an Anthropology of the Contemporary*.

Designs ranges over many topics, from the recounting of personal trajectories, historical debates, disciplinary tensions, and ruptures, to pedagogy, the ethnographic method, and experimental practice. Rather than chapters, the text is organized into seven dialogues, each of which roughly encompasses a particular theme. What is particularly interesting is that the dialogues never become didactic, but remain at a level of discourse that has the feel of an open and inquisitive conversation. From the vantage point of the first decade of the new millennium, the conversations look back on the tumultuous decades from the 1960s forward to sketch the landscape of the discipline as it was being reformulated. In this respect, *Designs* provides lessons in the anthropology's history while illuminating the ways in which the tensions and fissures of the previous decades created a space for discovery, inspiration, and an appreciation of the discipline in its present state. Both Rabinow and Marcus agreed that the tensions and frictions were productive and not unexpected: anthropology as a discipline encourages "strong feelings about public issues and the world" (2008: 23) as well as about developments, projects, and directions within the field.

Dialogues and Designs

In retrospect, what is striking about *Designs* is how the seven dialogues within the text capture an ongoing conversation between Rabinow and Marcus, occasionally joined by Faubion and Rees, as it evolved over time. From Dialogue I, where the conversation is dominated by *Writing Cultures: The Poetics and Politics of Ethnography* (Clifford & Marcus, 1986) to Dialogue VII, a summary that Rees suggested could be framed as a call for "a deparochialized" anthropology, we get the sense of "the considerable shifts of viewpoints" (Weber as cited Rabinow et al., 2008: 1) that the text encompasses. How anthropology has been reconceptualized not only reshaped the discipline and, albeit more slowly, the approach to teaching and learning anthropology, but also caused anthropologists to individually reevaluate their own work.

Dialogue I begins by laying out in great detail the personalities and events, and projects of the 1950s[10] that set the stage for discussing the impact of *Writing Culture* (Clifford & Marcus, 1986). A number of themes emerge that frame what was happening within the field during this period: the introspective focus of debates, the ethnocentric nature of engagement, and the rise of various schools and projects as people sought meaning in their work as anthropologists, and meaningful and relevant streams for their research. Particularly striking about the flurry of activities in the field at this time is *the crucial role of text* as the primary vehicle for communication. Thus, debates were waged behind the veil of the academy and were shrouded in language and conceptual jargon that made them extremely difficult for anyone outside the field to access.

In the Wake of Writing Culture: New Projects

Rabinow and Marcus both contributed chapters to *Writing Culture*, which Marcus described in retrospect as an "epistemological critique that puts its [anthropology's] very project in question" (2008: 30).

> *Writing Culture* was viewed in largely negative terms in anthropology. It did the job of opening up or of demolition, depending on how you look at it, without putting anything else in its place…Even though it addressed critically the problem of the Malinowskian encounter with the 'Other', it was still framed by that problem even if its moment had passed."
>
> *(2008: 30)*

What would come after would take shape around the definitive break that *Writing Culture* represented. The following six dialogues cover subsequent developments in anthropology and, through the constant "back and forth" of the exchange between Marcus and Rabinow, discuss the conceptual and methodological challenges that these developments posed for the practice of anthropology, questioning not only, "What is anthropology *today*?" but also, "What could it be? Where does it come from and in which ways might it develop?" (Rabinow et al., 2008: 115).

New projects and areas of engagement represent various turns in the post-1980s era. Rabinow and Marcus discuss ethnographic reflexivity, which *Writing Culture* did much to legitimize, the turn toward "self" and identity politics that Rabinow noted corresponded "to some degree with the 'collapse' – or whatever word would be better – of cultural wholes," and the *Public Culture* project, which Marcus saw as more influential and successful than either reflexivity or identity. Citing the significant contributions of *Public Culture* journal, Marcus noted that it "provided the ground for rethinking the whole idea of area studies." Rees added that the journal played an important role in formulating a cultural anthropology of globalization (Rabinow et al., 2008: 37), summing up the contributions of Appadurai and others who repositioned the culture concept and established it as central for understanding the flux of people and things in a globalized and increasingly digitally and physically connected world.

> If a globalized world is a culturally heterogeneous world, in which people and things are in flux, then 'cultural' anthropology has a major contribution to make for the understanding and conceptualization of a global cultural sphere or a cultural democracy.
>
> *(2008: 38)*

Other projects within this period include science and technology studies (STS), and medical anthropology. Yet what relates directly to the eventual emergence of design anthropology was the shift toward "objects and the objective."[11] Citing *The Social Life of Things* (Appadurai, 1986) that appeared in the same year as *Writing Culture*, Faubion noted "a shift of attention that has since snowballed and expanded its terrain." He noted how material culture and the built environment had regained their standing alongside people as relevant fieldwork subjects in terms of what they contribute to anthropological knowledge production.

> One cannot escape noticing a rehabilitation of material culture and cultural material as an entirely legitimate focus of analysis. Increasingly, objects are taking, if not center stage, at least as much of the stage in anthropology as people, and, with that shift, I think that one also sees the leaving behind of epistemological problems.
>
> *(2008: 38)*

Through the dialogues that follow the metaphor of *design* as an inspiration for moving anthropological practice toward the contemporary begins to take shape. Rabinow explains that "designs" are seen as a set of conceptual tools "for thinking through and practicing an anthropology of the contemporary" developed with the aim of "relating to and exploring the present conditions of anthropology" (2008: 11–12).

What It Means to Be "Contemporary"

In defining what it means to be "contemporary," Rabinow cites two meanings: the first is *temporal*, as in "existing or occurring at, or dating from, the same period of time as something or someone else." The second is, *historical* connotation that can be used to "both equate and differentiate the contemporary from the modern" (Rabinow et al., 2008: 57). The task of the *anthropology of the contemporary* is then to choose or find appropriate field sites, to document and analyze such assemblages in the process of their emergence, "to name them, to show their various effects and affects, and to thereby make them available for thought and critical reflection" (2008: 58).

Rabinow noted that being both close to things as they happen while at the same time preserving a critical distance represents a sense of "untimeliness"

(2008: 58). The quality of untimeliness, taken from Nietzsche's *Untimely Meditations* (1997), is "used to mark a critical distance from the present that seeks to establish a relationship to the present different from reigning opinion." This quality is sometimes referred to by anthropologists as "problematizing" a situation or phenomenon, and it remains essential to the practice of anthropology. To be "untimely" means not simply reporting the actual by being adjacent to it, but to both describe and interrogate it through analysis, "to think in a manner that leads to inquiry" (2008: 59). Distinctly anthropological inquiry provides something that other forms of social and cultural analysis pass over, which is what makes it a critical component and practice in design anthropology.

The authors of *Designs* deliver a heavy-hitting and illuminating critique of the discipline, providing a "conversation across generations" that delivers us to a plateau from which to view a multidimensional landscape of the past as well as glimpses from their vantage points of possible futures of a "contemporary" anthropology. During the dialogues there are points at which the authors seem to abandon the field only to return again to restate their concern "to explore possibilities for building bridges from the past to the present." Bridging entails not simply recognizing a past and a present period, but more precisely, distinctive traditional, modernity, and contemporary periods, seeing them not as static and opposed periods, but as paired dynamics. The contemporary, then, "is a moving image of modernity, moving through the recent past and near future in a space that gauges modernity as an ethos already becoming historical" (Rabinow et al., 2008: 11).

Bridging traditional and contemporary requires more than applying classical anthropological tropes such as ritual, magic, and exchange that are rooted in the literary form of what was and remains much of ethnographic writing. The power of tropes as rhetorical devices and frames has persisted. However, when they are applied in contemporary ethnographic contexts they can appear strikingly out of place which is usually because, without a deep understanding of the original work that produced them – the classical ethnographic works by the likes of Bronislaw Malinowski, E.E. Evans-Pritchard, Victor Turner, Claude Lévi-Strauss, Clifford Geertz, and others – tropes fall flat as frameworks. Efforts to retrieve and repurpose anthropological concepts, methods of inquiry, and processes of knowledge production are not wasted, even though they were shaped in research contexts and under conditions that were, on many but not all levels, radically different than what we know and do today. Rees observed,

> We seem to always return to the same point, namely the need to reconnect new research venues with the traditional or classical tropes of anthropology. The adjacent/untimely seems to offer such a connection insofar as it reminds us of the classical anthropological concept of 'being foreign.' We've been somewhere else and now, coming back from there, we are sensitive to the peculiarities of our own culture or can describe it with the eyes of others.

(2008: 62–63)

The Design Studio as an Analogy and a Model

Marcus raised the topic of design practice and the design studio (2008: 82–83) as a model for teaching, especially how to do fieldwork, as something between art and social science that fits with the projects and contexts of contemporary anthropological practice. Based on his experience in architectural design studios, he describes the design studio and practice of design critiques as "collaborative, in a mode designed to facilitate the process of invention, of learning, of analysis" (2008: 81–85).

My own experience in working with designers led me to a similar conclusion. Because anthropology, like design, is practice-oriented, it is a good candidate for incorporating something like the practices of the design studio. Rabinow notes that,

> It [anthropology] is not theory-driven, so there are embodied skills involved. What we lack, therefore, is a space of criticism, but one in which there is authority as in the lab meeting or the design studio. And there is plenty of authority and power in anthropology, but it's not given a function, it is not focused and it doesn't move.
>
> *(2008: 84)*

Equally important, the design studio model disrupts the assumptions that function as rarely challenged scripts that continue to implicitly organize anthropological work. The script reads that, "Anthropology is about ordinary people, about victims, sufferers, and the view from below, and so forth. One organizing element of this script is that analysis is secondary to politics, right?" (Rabinow et al., 2008: 90).

The analogy of the design studio persists as a promising model for a sort of training space that "could be a place in which students could be taught – could experience – how to anthropologize all the information that they have assembled on their particular topic before they actually begin fieldwork" (2008: 113). The design studio experience would equip students with an "anthropological toolkit" that would give them a certain "anthropological sensibility."

Today the design studio analogy has become a reality in emerging anthropological practices like design anthropology. Rather than the classic solitude of anthropological work, anthropologists are instead working collaboratively as members of pluridisciplinary project teams. They are engaging in critique. In these projects it is not the singular theoretical or technical brilliance of any one disciplinary team member that matters. What matters instead is credibility that comes from collectively producing and maintaining what Rabinow and Marcus call "high quality work."

Adaptive Strategies

Throughout this chapter, the aim has been to capture what the authors of *Designs* refer to as the *residual, dominant,* and the *emergent,* the three categories that constitute the present as a dynamic phenomenon (Rabinow et al., 2008: 95). In order to represent the dynamics that are in play, all three must be present in the "anthropology of the contemporary" that the authors envision. The three categories create a sort of prism, each a different facet, which, when looking through it, illuminates a different angle on the story, a different overall picture, and yet unrealized dimensions. Incorporating these perspectives is essential to the complex multisited design of research that characterizes much of contemporary fieldwork and ethnography.

The final dialogues include a discussion between Rabinow, Marcus, and Faubion about time compression and the impact of the accelerated speed of research, an important topic in contemporary fieldwork. Rabinow is adamant that in order to remain pertinent to the contemporary world, anthropologists *must* figure out how to speed up some aspects of its practices of inquiry. Yes, but only *certain aspects* while "Others remain in need always of more sustained, inferential, and indirect attention" (2008: 95). This means paying attention to the "micro-processes and/or everyday life," work that cannot be rushed: "To do anthropology it takes a long time to figure out what is significant about what is going on, because what's going on is not obvious and often not quite what is being talked about explicitly" (2008: 95). The issues of speed and temporality are critical in the ways that anthropology is practiced today, especially in the compressed short-term engagements of commercial and organizational ethnographic projects. New forms of data collection, such as streaming video and sensor-based data feeds, have become common in research designs. These types of data are problematic in that they are not experienced directly by the researcher and can be taken out of context, especially for client briefings. Examples of how this challenge is being met in the commercial sector by design firms, for example Iota Partners[12] and others, has been documented in multiple sources.[13]

The conversation shifts to how a focus on "the contemporary," as a time closely connected to the present, particularly in relation to modern time, has impacted anthropological writing, especially the ethnographic monograph. Monographs, once the primary vehicle for transmitting anthropological knowledge, are most interesting "as symptoms or indices of change" (Rabinow et al., 2008: 97). Tales are still important, Marcus maintains, but more so in the reflexivity of "shoptalk," and stories we listen to and exchange within the boundaries of our professional culture. The significant stories are not so much about "the fieldwork experience bounded by the Malinowskian scene of encounter, but more broadly about the design of research" (2008: 97). Because of the multisited nature of contemporary field work and the involvement of teammates from a diverse range of disciplinary backgrounds (2008: 69), these are not stories that the anthropologist should be telling alone.

The implications for teaching anthropology are clear: reading ethnographies as exemplars is a grossly inadequate mode of training for students today. Based on the discussions that started with *Writing Culture* as the critique of traditional ethnography, and continuing through the evaluation of the state of ethnographic monographs in the present day, Marcus concludes "...as we have discussed, ethnographies are anything but exemplars today. Rather, they are to be read as experiments, for their bits and pieces" (2008: 100).

Deparochializing Anthropology

The final dialogue consists of a summing up of the previous conversations that Rees suggested can be framed around the concept of "deparochialization." A "deparochialized discipline," Rees explains, is one that is diverse, heterogeneous, and "impossible to reduce to one or two key paradigms. It is open and vivid and moving" (Rabinow et al., 2008: 105). The demise of the culture concept coincided with the demotion of anthropology's "father figures" such as Eric Wolf, David Schneider, and Marshall Sahlins, and corresponded to changes in the question of culture and its role in anthropology. The time of thinking of culture as "separate islands of culture" or as "cultural wholes" that were unique and distinct, was over. And yet the idea of culture remains, but in a different sense than it was conceived in traditional anthropology. Faubion makes the distinction between "culture and the cultural"[14]: culture as the concept of "bounded wholes" would go, but the *cultural* "as a constitutive dimension of human life, as one of the planes – an open plane, to be sure – of which it is always composed" would remain (2008: 106).

This is a critical distinction, but one that is not particularly easy to decipher for anyone that is not steeped in the debates within anthropology since the 1950s. Today, the idea of "culture" seems to retain meaning for many people and has been appropriated by other disciplines. But for many decades now, anthropologists have *not* been studying isolated "islands of culture;" it can easily be argued that this was actually never the case. The traditional practice of *studying a culture* became meaningless. However, *the cultural* as one plane or dimension of human life – "the cultural as a marker of difference" – continues to be a rich source of elements that are, according to Marcus, distinctly susceptible to semiotic[15] analysis. In other words, we can understand cultural elements – the aspects of material and symbolic culture – through the study of how meaning is constructed and communicated in concrete venues through signs and symbols and the objects or ideas that they reference. While the signs or symbols implicit in objects are sometimes more accessible, much of our understanding is obscured because symbolic communication is not overtly visible, residing in what Faubion describes as the "domain of the imponderabilia" that constitutes much of everyday life: the tone of voice, the local reference, the glance, and the level of intimate engagement that provides the ability to distinguish between a wink and a blink. This competency is only accessible to those who are intimately connected and yet somehow stand apart. Rabinow suggests that "the concept of the cultural allows one to approach or assess the object of analysis better and in a more adequate way than the idea of culture, *because culture somehow requires that everything else is subsumed under it* [italics added]" (2008: 110).

Although many of anthropology's traditional tropes have fallen into disuse, and while the "norms and forms" of practice have been transformed, the discipline has adapted and evolved, often by turning the lens of critical analysis on itself. We have examples of how the design studio that the authors of *Designs* envisioned might be realized in anthropological pedagogy[16] and practice today. The final sections of this chapter focus on the last of three texts that frame this chapter. Not to be taken as exemplars, they form a web of ideas that represent "continuity across change" (Rabinow et al., 2008: 47), each piece providing a window into a particular point in time through the voice or voices of highly regarded individuals in the field.

Anthropological Relocations and the Limits of Design

Anthropologists have witnessed the rise of new subfields in what Lucy Suchman (2011: 15) called "a turn toward 'home', understood as the value, even urgency, of anthropological inquiry into locations characterized by their cultural familiarity and their political and economic centrality." The field's "relocation" relative to design and innovation is one example in which anthropologists are engaged in both inventing new forms of practice while simultaneously undertaking critique. Suchman's reference to location encompasses the categories of residual, dominant, and emergent: "the concept of location, as it has been articulated in the context of anthropology's reflections on its history and positioning as a field and in relation to shifting engagements with contemporary technoscience, political, and ethical problems" (2011: 3). Situating her arguments relative to those of several of her contemporaries (Mau & Leonard, 2004; Rabinow et al., 2008), Suchman draws on her extensive engagement in professional technology design as well as her day-to-day experiences as a resident of Palo Alto in California's Silicon Valley. Rather than seeing design as a model for anthropology's future (referring to Rabinow et al., 2008), she proposes "instead that design and innovation are best positioned as problematic objects for an anthropology of the contemporary" (2011: 3).

Suchman defined her position as one that maintains an "interest in ways of theorizing change, breaks, ruptures, and the new that do not rely on singular origins, or definite moments of invention, or trajectories of progressive development." She shares the commitment to working across disciplinary boundaries and with other practitioners in other locations, but also states "that we need less a reinvented anthropology *as* (or for) design than a critical anthropology *of* design" (2011: 3).

Suchman and the authors of *Designs* were coming from very different experiences with and of design. For Marcus and Rabinow (2008: 81–85), from their vantage point in the academic environment, design presented an alternative to traditional anthropological pedagogy that met the requirements of an anthropology of the contemporary. For Suchman, living and working in an epicenter of professional technology design, design was not a model for an anthropology of the contemporary, but a problematic object. Reconciling these opposing viewpoints is one of the challenges that design anthropologists continue to face.

Design: Anthropology's Future or Problematic Object?

In part, Suchman was responding to the authors of *Designs for an Anthropology of the Contemporary*, but also to what she regarded as *design hubris*, pointing to Bruce Mau's *Massive Change* project (Mau & Leonard, 2004) as an example. She refers to *Massive Change* as a "particularly encompassing expression" of an orientation that marks a technological society (Barry, 2001),

> an orientation that privileges change and then figures change as technological innovation (201). Innovation, in turn, is embedded within a broader cultural imaginary that posits a world that is always lagging, always in need of being brought up to date through the intercessions of those trained to shape it: a world, in sum, in need of design.
>
> *(2011: 5)*

It's understandable why Suchman chose to use *Massive Change* as an expression of the orientation Barry described, especially based on the implications of its title. Published in 2004, *Massive Change*, was an expression of the new recognition of the power of design and its central position in the complex systems and assemblages that make up the contemporary world. It was also a project of the Institute without Boundaries (IwB)[17] and included as contributors a cadre of professionals from a wide range of design subfields and other disciplines. The text is a graphically rich design project published by Phaidon Press, overlaying stark photos of (often abandoned or failed) designed products and systems with quotations such as the following that appears over a photo of the aftermath of jet fuel tank fires caused by Super Typhoon Pongsona, Apra Harbor, Guam, December 2002.

> Accidents, disasters, crisis. When systems fail we become temporarily conscious of the extraordinary force and power of design, and the effects that it generates. Every accident provides a brief moment of awareness of real life, what is actually happening, and our dependence on the underlying systems of design.
>
> *(Mau & Leonard, 2004: front matter)*

Statements that open each chapter, such as "We will create urban shelter for the entire world population." (Mau & Leonard, 2004: 30) are particularly emblematic of *design hubris* to which Suchman refers. Highlighting an excerpt from the text, she blasts the attitude that positions "design as one of the world's most powerful forces", which implies that "'it' now replaces 'us' at the beginning of something unprecedented and global. This announced tipping point, of past and future action, is a hallmark of new things…[that] promises that 'we' can now 'plan and produce desired outcomes through design' at an unprecedented scale" (Suchman, 2011: 5).

Suchman traces what she calls *design hubris*, the statement "Now we can do anything, what will we do?" (Mau & Leonard, 2004), to the publication of *The Sciences of the Artificial* (Simon, 1969), the decade of the 1970s, and the emergence of professional design. Simon's vision of design as moving from "soft" skills to "tough analytic doctrine" (Simon cited 1969: 113 by Suchman, 2011: 5) was challenged over 40 years later by Margolin (2002) who noted that design as descended from Simon's vision was more focused on models of the design process than on a "critical theory of practice" (Margolin, 2002: 237 cited by Suchman, 2011: 5–6). Rather than a science of design, Margolin envisioned design as a social practice, one that Suchman noted would incorporate "history, theory, and criticism as central rather than peripheral elements, including critical examination of conceptions of design theory inherited from Simon and his followers" (2011: 6).[18]

Suchman made clear that in writing about "the limits of design" she did not intend to negate the value of projects in which the goal was to "address pressing problems or to explore untried possibilities." She argued instead that design, like anthropology, "needs to acknowledge the specificity of its place, to locate itself as one (albeit multiple) figure and practice of change." Citing the history of professional design since the mid-twentieth century and its effects and legacy, Suchman highlights a conception of the design method "that systematically obscures the questions that anthropology might find central to a consideration of what constitutes transformative change and how it happens." She notes that another limitation of design rests on the presupposition that method entails "an open horizon of competencies and contingencies" that can be drawn upon as a situation requires, but which cannot be fully accounted for or specified. In other words, she argues, *conventional design methods* focus on aspects that are considered relevant to the designer, but would ignore other aspects that an anthropologist would find compelling and in need of articulation.

Suchman's critique reminds us that the history of a field of practice, as well as the ways in which its practitioners position their work in relation to the overwhelming array of complex contemporary problems, *does matter.* Acknowledging this as fact requires a stepping back to consider how design anthropology – and design itself – has responded to these criticisms. Before turning our attention to critiques of contemporary anthropology, in particular, design anthropology, we must understand the conditions and events that occurred within the field of design to make sense of its encounter with the social sciences, and in particular, with anthropology.

Notes

1 Ingold argued that the term ethnography has been so overused both within anthropology and in other disciplines that it has lost much of its meaning. He argues against attributing "ethnographicness" to encounters with the people, things, and places where we do our research. Instead, we should preserve the meaning of the term as referring to a distinct literary genre.

2 See, for example, *"New Proposals for Anthropologists"* (Gough, 1968).

3 Dell Hymes cited Lévi-Strauss's pronouncement in her introduction to *Reinventing Anthropology* (1969: 3).

4 Although as anthropology graduate students we engaged in discussion about the disappearance of indigenous populations, these discussions, along with our personal research interests and the guidance of faculty mentors, had much to do with how we chose our research field sites.

5 https://en.wikipedia.org/wiki/Bureau_of_American_Ethnology.

6 Lévi-Strauss noted that the volumes were selling for $2 to $3 per item. He eventually collected all but one of the 48 volumes.

7 Referring to his time at the University of Chicago during the 1960s, Rabinow reflected that, "On the philosophic side, the main influence for me was Richard McKeon" (2008: 19). Lévi-Strauss was also teaching at Chicago during this time. Rabinow noted, "The Strauss circle never tempted me," to which McKeon was "fundamentally opposed," but he was fascinated by the man himself.

8 Foster, G.M. 1959. The Potter's Wheel: An Analysis of Idea and Artifact in Invention. *Southwestern Journal of Anthropology*, 15(2), 99–117.

9 Universität Tübingen, located in Tübingen, Baden-Württemberg, Germany, was founded in 1477 and is one of the oldest universities in Europe.

10 Clifford Geertz is described as "at the forefront of American cultural anthropology from the later 1960s to the early 1980s." Major funding from the Ford Foundation supported collaborative programs such as Harvard's Department of Social Relations and those at MIT.

11 The entry of objects into human networks and the conceptualization of objects as actors was proposed by Bruno Latour, Thomas Hughes, John Law, and others engaged in science and technology studies and the sociology of science and technology (Bijker, Hughes, & Pinch, 1999).

12 Iota Partners + Sapient has developed methods and devices to mine data from the Internet of Things (IoT), "using sensor-based data to disrupt an ecosystem." Their work will be discussed in the following chapters as an example of how design anthropology is inventing new methods and practices. www.iota-partners.com/.

13 Many blogs, listservs, and other online resources provide forums for discussing issues around the challenges of project work and time compression. Examples include the listserv Anthrodesign, Anthropologizing.com (Amy Santee), the anthropology Slack channel, anthropologists.slack.com, and EPIC People, www.epicpeople.org/.

14 "Writing against Culture" (Abu-Lughod, 1991).

15 "The science of communication studied through the interpretation of signs and symbols as they operate in various fields, esp. language," *Oxford English Dictionary* (2003).

16 Design anthropology programs, usually at the graduate level, are operating in both Europe and the United States. See Chapter 4 which references several of these programs.

17 The Institute without Boundaries (IwB) was founded in 2003 by the School of Design at George Brown College in Toronto in collaboration with Canadian designer and architect, Bruce Mau. Its mission is "Fostering collaboration between disciplines to create innovative local solutions to 21st century global challenges." (Accessed January 16, 2017) http://institutewithoutboundaries.ca/about-us/overview/.

18 Both *The Sciences of the Artificial* (Simon, 1969) and *The Politics of the Artificial* (Margolin, 2002) are covered in the following chapter.

References

Abu-Lughod, Lila. 1991. Writing Against Culture. In R.G. Fox (Ed.), *Recapturing Capturing Anthropology: Working in the Present*, 50–59. Santa Fe: School for American Research.

Appadurai, Arjun. (Ed.). 1986. *The Social Life of Things: Commodities in Cultural Perspective*. Santa Fe: School for American Research.

Baba, Marietta. 2006. Anthropology and Business. In H.J. Brix (Ed.), *Encyclopedia of Anthropology*, vol. 1, 83–117. Thousand Oaks, CA: Sage Publications.

Barry, Andrew. 2001. *Political Machines: Governing a Technological Society*. London: Athlone.

Bijker, Wiebe E., Thomas P. Hughes, and Trevor Pinch (Eds.). 1999. *The Social Construction of Technological Systems: New Directions in the Sociology and History of Technology*. Cambridge, MA: MIT Press.

Blomberg, Jeanette and Mark Burrell. 2009. An Ethnographic Approach to Design. In A. Sears and J.A. Jacko (Eds.), *Human-Computer Interaction: Development Process*, 964–986. Boca Raton, FL: CRC Press.

Cefkin, Melissa (Ed.). 2010. *Ethnography and the Corporate Encounter: Reflections on Research in and of the Corporation*. New York: Berghahn Books.

Clifford, James and George E. Marcus (Eds.). 1986. *Writing Cultures: The Poetics and Politics of Ethnography*. Los Angeles: University of California Press.

Gough, Kathleen. 1968. New Proposals for Anthropologists. *Current Anthropology*, 9(5), 403–407.

Gunn, W. 2008. Learning to ask naïve questions with IT product design students. *Arts and Humanities in Higher Education*, 7(3), 323–336.

Halse, Joachim. 2013. Ethnographies of the Possible. In W. Gunn, T. Otto, and R.C. Smith (Eds.), *Design Anthropology: Theory and Practice*, 180–196. New York: Bloomsbury.

Hymes, Dell (Ed.). 1969. *Reinventing Anthropology*. New York: Vintage.

Ingold, T. 2014. That's Enough about Ethnography! *HAU: Journal of Ethnographic Theory*, 4(1), 383–395. doi:10.14318/hau4.1.021

Jordan, Ann T. 2003. *Business Anthropology*. Prospect Heights, IL: Waveland Press, Inc.

Kapferer, Bruce. 2010. Introduction: In the Event-toward an Anthropology of Generic Moments. *Social Analysis*, 54(3), 1–27.

Kilbourn, Kyle. 2013. Tools and Movements of Engagement: Design Anthropology's Style of Knowing. In W. Gunn, T. Otto, and R.C. Smith (Eds.), *Design Anthropology: Theory and Practice*. New York: Bloomsbury.

Lévi-Strauss, Claude. 1966. Anthropology: Its Achievements and Future. *Current Anthropology*, 7(2), 124–127.

Margolin, Victor. 2002. *Politics of the Artificial: Essays on Design and Design Studies*. Chicago: University of Chicago Press.

Mau, Bruce and Jennifer Leonard. 2004. *Massive Change*. New York: Phaidon.

Mayo, Elton. 1945. *The Social Problems of an Industrial Civilization*. Andover, MA: Andover Press.

Miller, Christine. 2017. Owning It: Evolving Ethics in Design and Design Research. In T. de Waal Malefyt and R.J. Morais (Eds.), *Ethics in the Anthropology of Business*, 87–102. New York: Routledge.

Nietzsche, Friedrich W. 1997. *Untimely Meditations*. New York: Cambridge University Press.

Otto, Ton and Rachel C. Smith (Eds.). 2013. Design Anthropology: A Distinct Way of Knowing. In W. Gunn, T. Otto, and R.C. Smith (Eds.), *Design Anthropology: Theory and Practice*, 1–29. New York: Bloomsbury.

Rabinow, Paul. 2003. *Anthropos Today: Reflections on Modern Equipment*. Princeton, NJ: Princeton University Press.

Rabinow, Paul, George E. Marcus, James Faubion, and Tobias Rees (Eds.). 2008. *Designs for an Anthropology of the Contemporary*. Durham, NC: Duke University Press.

Rees, Tobias. 2008a. "Design" and "Design Studio". In P. Rabinow, G.E. Marcus, J. Faubion, and T. Rees (Eds.), *Designs for an Anthropology of the Contemporary*, 115–121. Durham, NC: Duke University Press.

Rees, Tobias. 2008b. "Introduction: Today, What is Anthropology?" In P. Rabinow, G.E. Marcus, J. Faubion, and T. Rees (Eds.), *Designs for an Anthropology of the Contemporary*, 1–12. Durham, NC: Duke University Press.

Schwartzman, Helen B. 1993. *Ethnography in Organizations*, vol. 27. In J. van Manaan, P.K.Manning, M.L. Miller (Series Eds.). Qualitative Research Methods Series. Newbury Park, CA: Sage Publications.

Simon, Herbert. 1969. *The Sciences of the Artificial*. Cambridge, MA: MIT Press.

Suchman, Lucy. 2011. Anthropological Relocations and the Limits of Design. *Annual Review of Anthropology*, 40, 1–18.

Tunstall, Elizabeth. 2013. Decolonizing Design Innovation: Design Anthropology, Critical Anthropology and Indigenous Knowledge. In W. Gunn, T. Otto, and R.C. Smith (Eds.), *Design Anthropology: Theory and Practice*, 232–250. New York: Bloomsbury.

van Veggel, Rob J.F.M. 2005. Where the Two Sides of Ethnography Collide. *Design Issues*, 21(3), 3–16.

Wasson, Christina. 2000. Ethnography in the Field of Design. *Human Organization*, 59(4), 377–388.

2
DESIGN ROOTS

Introduction

> The history of design is not merely a history of objects. It is a history of the changing views of subject matter held by designers and the concrete objects conceived, planned, and produced as expressions of those views. One could go further and say that the history of design history is a record of the design historians' views regarding what they conceive to be the subject matter of design.
>
> *(Buchanan, 1992: 19)*

As in the previous chapter, Chapter 2 references particular texts that are positioned as facets through which to achieve two broad aims: first, to sketch the historical trajectory of each field; second, to explore the legacies and discourse that facilitated the transdisciplinary confluence that is design anthropology. The goal in this chapter is to trace the movements within design that led to a space where it was possible – and, in fact, became necessary – for designers to integrate method and theory from other disciplines in order to respond to the challenges they were asked (or volunteered) to solve.

The texts that are referenced in this chapter highlight particular issues around which conversations emerged that were critical to the evolution of the field. They serve as a "reading" of the contexts in which design practice was evolving. Although each text represents a specific point in time, a particular agenda, and point of view, there are threads of discourse – both supporting and conflicting – that connect the texts across time and space. The texts are not intended to present a linear progression of the evolution of design. They are not presented in sequential order. Instead, they illuminate multiple strands of discourse and thought about design theory and practice in the contemporary world that served to advance particular aims and practices, some of which have combined to create new fields (Margolin, 2002).

The opening sections approach design as it entered the final decades of the twentieth century, a period during which professional design, characterized by an increasing separation from fine arts, craft work, and the trades, was emerging. New movements in intellectual thought were challenging the prevailing paradigm of modernism that greatly influenced art and culture from the early decades of the twentieth century. *The Sciences of the Artificial* (Simon, 1996) and *The Politics of the Artificial* (Margolin, 2002) reveal a discourse around constructions of the natural and the artificial that have been referenced and critiqued by authors within and outside design. These texts have important implications for contemporary design and provide a perspective from which we can investigate their role in the paradigm of future-making and innovation.

Significance and Implications for Anthropology

For anthropology, the implications of shifting paradigms within the field of design lie in the turn from object-centered to user-centered or human-centered design. The exploration of these texts considers Lucy Suchman's call for "a critical anthropology *of* design" (2011: 3) while recognizing the argument (Gatt & Ingold, 2013) that Suchman's proposal is

> too limiting, insofar as it narrows the scope of anthropology, in relation to design, to an essentially ethnographic project, and one, moreover, that in its focus on the emergence of design science – specifically in the United States in the second half of the twentieth century – is of an exceedingly constricted historical and geographical reach.
>
> *(2013: 140)*

Both positions embody significant concerns. Suchman argues that "like anthropology, design needs to acknowledge the specificities of its place, to locate itself as one (albeit multiple) figure and practice of transformation." As previously noted, in describing the limits of design, she draws our attention to the ways "in which conventional design methods are (necessarily) silent on matters that anthropology would be interested in articulating" (2008: 3). Texts that are referenced in the following sections suggest why calls for critical design practice, from both within the field and externally, are so urgent. To Gatt and Ingold's point, the geographical contexts in which design emerged as a field of professional practice, specifically in the United States and in Europe, are distinctly different. This suggests that "an anthropology of design" would entail a much more comprehensive study that would include multiple geographical contexts. Furthermore, Gatt and Ingold argue that: "The trouble with an 'anthropology of' formula, whether applied to design or to any other human activity, is that it turns the activity in question into an object of analysis" (2013: 140). This makes it nearly impossible to perceive the activity as a dynamic and continually evolving space of invention, improvisation, and innovation.

> Our aim, to the contrary, is to restore design to the heart of anthropology's disciplinary practice. This is not to advocate a return to cognitivism. But it is to suggest that there are other ways of thinking about design than in terms of setting determinant ends in advance, and other ways of thinking about anthropology than as a description and analysis of what has already come to pass.
>
> *(2013: 140)*

This aim implies the reimagining of both fields,

> an open-ended concept of design that makes allowances for hopes and dreams and for the improvisatory dynamic of the everyday, and for a discipline of anthropology conceived as a speculative inquiry into the conditions and possibilities of human life.
>
> *(2013: 141)*

Gatt and Ingold refer to this concept for rethinking design and anthropology as "correspondence," a practice of active engagement with the world. They propose design anthropology – "anthropology-by-means-of-design" – as a practice "that seeks to correspond with, rather than to describe, the lives it follows" (2013: 144). This reformulated concept of practice extends the role of the researcher in the field from participant observer to "participant interventionist": both a researcher *for* a project and a researcher *of* a project (2013: 51).

The texts featured in the following sections present an opportunity to trace the development of theory and practice in design from a perspective that allows us to think critically, but also to consider design's vast potential. The next section introduces the first selection, *The Sciences of the Artificial*, in which Simon (1996) proposes his concept of the "science of design." In this collection of lectures and essays Simon's draws a sharp distinction between "natural" and "artificial" sciences. Through broad generalizations, he constructs a definition of design based on his concept of artificial sciences, such as engineering and psychology that apply the natural sciences, for example, physics, mathematics, biology, and botany. According to Simon, the natural sciences are concerned with describing the world as it is and understanding how it works whereas the work of the artificial sciences is to apply knowledge of the natural world to consider how the world *might* be: the domain of invention and the world of design.

The Sciences of the Artificial: Rationality and the Science of Design

The Sciences of the Artificial was first published in 1969 with later editions in 1981 and 1996. In this text, Simon extends the concept of design to all "professional fields," including engineering, medicine, and management. With the trend towards the professionalization and formalization of these and other fields well underway, Simon's theme of rationality, in particular what Herbert Marcuse (1964) describes as "technological rationality," resonates with the growing dominance of statistical analysis, operations research, and systems design and the rise of the post-World War II military-industrial complex. Rationality and its limits are underlying themes in *The Sciences of the Artificial*. Simon equates rational thought or behavior with "utility maximizing" (1996: 39), utility in the economic sense being "a measure of preferences"[1] over some set of goods or options.

In the essay "The Science of Design: Creating the Artificial" Simon states,

> Engineers are not the only professional designers. Everyone designs who devises courses of action aimed at changing existing situations into preferred ones. The intellectual activity that produces material artifacts is no different fundamentally from the one that prescribes remedies for a sick patient or the one that devises a new sales program for a company or a social welfare policy for a state. Design, so constructed, is the core of all professional training; it is the principal mark that distinguishes the professions from the sciences.
>
> *(1996: 111)*

Simon conceived of design as an *artificial science* and a key component of "professional activity" in fields including business, architecture, engineering, medicine, education, law, and journalism. According to Simon, these fields are by nature open to change; they are distinct from the natural sciences – mathematics, biology, physics, and other scientific fields that are concerned with "how things are and how they work" (1969: 111). He posits that natural science fields rely on standard or "ordinary" forms of logic: deductive and inductive reasoning. On the other hand, the fields that Simon refers to as the "sciences of the artificial," those in which design plays a key role, are concerned with "how things *ought to be* [italics added], with devising artifacts to attain goals" (1996: 112).

Simon argued that design required a different type of logic, one that is able to consider possible worlds and probabilities, the logic of *how might we?* Many years before Simon, the American logician, mathematician, scientist, and philosopher, Charles Sanders Peirce (1839–1914) conceptualized this type of reasoning as abductive logic, the logic of what *might* be true. Peirce's (1877) concept of abductive reasoning allows for leaps of abduction that open possible solution spaces. Today, abductive logic is considered to be at the heart of the design process or "design thinking." Interestingly, Simon does not mention abductive reasoning as an alternative form of reasoning in design, possibly, according to Roger Martin (2009: 65), because Peirce was discredited later in his career.

Herbert Simon in Context

Herbert Simon was an American political scientist, economist, sociologist, psychologist, and computer scientist. During his long career as an interdisciplinary scholar, he received many notable awards, including the American Psychological

Association Award for Distinguished Scientific Contributions to Psychology in 1969, the Nobel Prize in Economics in 1978, and the National Medal for Science in 1986. His belief that human behavior could be studied scientifically led him to develop the theory of *bounded rationality*, which posits that our ability to make rational decisions is limited by three factors: the information available to us, our cognitive capacity, and the time frame in which a decision needs to be made (Gigerenzer & Selten, 2002). Simon's concept of *satisficing* explains that, as decision makers, we make decisions that are the best we can manage at any given time – a *satisfactory* decision – rather than the decision that might be optimal (Simon, 1956). Decisions that "satisfice" are good enough.

Simon distinguishes between two "sciences": natural sciences – the world as it is – including biology, botany, anatomy, physics, and mathematics that are subject to natural law, those which give natural phenomenon "an air of necessity." Artificial sciences – engineering, medicine, business, painting, and architecture – are "concerned not with the necessary but with the contingent – not with how things are but with how they might be – in short, with design" (Simon, 1996: xii).

Simon defined the natural science disciplines by referring to their historic and traditional tasks "to teach about natural things: how they are and how they work" (Simon, 1996: 110). In contrast, the task of the sciences of the artificial is "to devise courses of action aimed at changing existing conditions." Simon argued that the cognitive processes involved in producing a material artifact are *fundamentally not different* from those required to engineer a bridge or to plan a policy or develop a business strategy: each of these activities involves design. Consequently, education and training in the *professional disciplines* of engineering, business, education, law, and medicine "are all centrally concerned with the process of design" (Simon, 1996: 111).

What are the Implications for Anthropology?

At the same time that this position raises the significance of design as a professional field, what Simon posits is problematic for anthropology relative to its claim, and at times a tentative position as a natural science. If we accept Simon's reasoning and place anthropology in the domain of natural (albeit human) science, then the task of anthropology is to produce a scientific account of human societies. Positioned as such, this task is essentially descriptive and interpretive: to describe how "things" are and to interpret how they work. In its traditional and conventional form, this is what anthropology has been. However, the conditions that resulted in a reevaluation and subsequent reinventions of the discipline and the resulting schism between "applied" anthropology and the traditional or conventional form of the discipline raise the question as to how anthropology would be positioned in Simon's scheme. The emergence of transdisciplinary subfields, such as design anthropology, challenge fundamental tenets of the discipline, a topic that is discussed at length in following chapters.

Simon's distinction between natural and artificial sciences provides a simplified understanding of the relationship between basic science and the domain of the man-made, or artificial sciences. He arrives at this understanding by abstracting and applying what Susan Leigh Star (1989) refers to as the "process of deletion" to factors that make problems unmanageable. Star references Simon's (1973) distinction between "ill-structured" problems (ISP) and "well-structured" problems (WSP), stating that the process of transforming ill-structured problems into well-structured ones is essential in learning to do scientific work.

> Scientists break ill-structured problems into pieces that they work on *as if* they were well-structured, in order to get the work done. Creating well-structured problems requires ignoring complexity: uncertainties in the environment, subjects' or participants' reactions, unforeseen interaction effects. In order to actually do the research, lines and boundaries must be drawn around complications, implications, and exceptions. Goals, images, and tasks simple enough to manage are developed.
>
> *(Star, 1989: 189)*

Diana Forsythe (1999: 143) argued that this process of deleting factors that contribute to complexity renders sociality and communicative work "invisible." However, these factors are at the heart of both anthropology and user-centered design.

By broadly defining design as the activity shared by all professional fields and by positioning it in the domain of the artificial, Simon established rationality as the design's guiding principle, privileging the technical over the artistic and intuitive.

Understanding Artifacts and Systems: The Dichotomy of Inner and Outer Environments

Simon makes a critical distinction between the *internal environment*, "the substance and organization of the artifact itself," and the *external environment*, "the surrounding in which it operates." He notes that "this way of viewing artifacts applies equally well to many things that are not man-made – to all things in fact that can be regarded as adapted to some situation; and in particular, it applies to the living systems that have evolved through the forces of organic evolution" (Simon, 1996: 6). The influence of early system thinking and Western science are evident. Richard Buchanan (1998: 14) notes the difference between the early form of systems thinking that "was fundamentally materialistic and reductive in orientation, despite a concern for wholes." Wholes in this case were treated as material: "*things* or information treated as a *thing*." Without referring directly to Simon, Buchanan describes this perspective: "This form of systems thinking was fundamentally concerned with the organization of means and offered only an anticipation of the deeper challenge of determining circumstances and ends." Later forms of design thinking began to emphasize the role of the social and the influence of people in determining how systems work. Buchanan cites the quality movement "as a form of high-end systems engineering" noting that "the radical feature of this movement was not, as it is sometimes suggested, a focus on statistical measures, but a rediscovery of collective human agency within organizations" (1998: 14).

explain the relationship between internal and external environments, Simon makes a comparison between an airplane and a bird, observing that a theory explaining the internal workings of the airplane (its power plant or motor), the external environment (conditions within the atmosphere at different altitudes), and the relation between internal and external environments draws on the natural sciences. A theory of how a bird is able to fly also relies on natural science for explanation. Accordingly, Simon argues, both airplanes and birds can be analyzed by methods of natural science "without any particular attention to purpose or adaptation, without reference to the interface between what I have called the inner and outer environments. After all, their behavior is governed by natural law just as fully as the behavior of anything else" (1996: 7).

According to Simon, the role of *rationality* in the sciences of human behavior is analogous to the role played by *natural selection* in evolutionary biology. Thus he posits that this explanation (conveniently) "demands an understanding mainly of the external or outer environment." Understanding the complexities of the inner environment is not necessary in order to predict the behavior of any complex system, such as a business organization. So, for example, Simon argues that

> If we know of a business organization only that it is a profit-maximizing system, we can often predict how its behavior will change if we change its environment. We can sometimes make this prediction…without detailed assumptions about the adaptive mechanism, the decision-making apparatus that constitutes the inner environment of the business firm.
>
> *(1996: 9)*

Simon justifies the need to ignore the inner workings of a complex system in predicting its behavior. Instead, the focus and goal of a complex system is to adapt the means – the inner – to the outer external environment with the objective of maximizing utility. According to Simon, the artificial world is "centered precisely on this interface" between inner and outer. How is the adaptation of means to goals brought about? Central to this question is "the process of design itself." Hence, the "logic of design" serves as a paradigm for *imperative logic* and a prescribed set of rules for achieving this objective.

The Emergence of Professional Design

Positioning Simon's broad definition of design and his proposal for a "science of design" in the context of his life and times contributed to the development of professional design, which by the 1970s was flourishing both in Europe and in the United States. Many designers – architects, industrial, and graphic designers – achieved celebrity status in the United States. Designers of this time were considered heralds of "the modern." During this period, Charles and Ray Eames designed the Eames Lounge Chair Wood (LCW), distinctively modern in sleek molded plywood, which went into production in 1946.[2] Beyond designing objects, they developed projects utilizing multiple media. In architecture, Frank Lloyd Wright was widely recognized for his innovative use of materials,[3] the distinctive Prairie School and later, Organic[4] architectural styles, and structures such as his final architectural project, the Solomon R. Guggenheim Museum in New York City.[5] Many other designers of this period achieved international recognition, including architects Mies Van der Rohe (1886–1969), Le Corbusier (Charles-Édouard Jeanneret-Gris [1887–1965]), and Walter Gropius (1883–1969), the first director of the Bauhaus that existed in Germany between 1919 and 1933.

Along with celebrity designers, a new wave of design movements was arriving on the scene. Schools of design were established across Europe and the United States. The Ulm School (1953–1968),[6] greatly influenced by the German Bauhaus movement (1919–1933),[7] and the Institute of Design at the Illinois Institute of Technology, founded by László Moholy-Nagy from the Bauhaus, are two of many examples. During and after the war, many of the Bauhaus designers relocated to the United States. In 1961, two Ulm graduates carried the Ulm model to the design school at Auburn University in Alabama where the user-centered systems design process was integrated into the design curriculum and influenced generations of designers.

By the time *The Sciences of the Artificial* was published in 1969, professional design was well-established in studios and in design schools and universities in the United States, including the Massachusetts Institute of Technology (MIT), Harvard, and Carnegie Mellon. Now clearly distinct from the fine arts, craftwork, and trades that relied on a tradition of apprenticeship design, was established as a professional field based on a formal system of credentials that were acquired through a prescribed course of study at an accredited institution. Much like trade guilds, professional design organizations were established to represent and protect the interests of credentialed practitioners. The process of professionalization created "occupational closure" that effectively barred nonaccredited individuals and amateurs from entering the field. The professionalization of design was also associated with gender politics that implicitly or explicitly restricted the profession to a single gender. Design, and especially industrial design, has traditionally been a male-dominated profession, although this is changing as new subdisciplines such as service design and design management have emerged. The shift is evident in student populations; however, it is not uncommon today to find that the faculty members of many design departments are male.

The Politics of the Artificial: Essays on Design and Design Studies

In *The Politics of the Artificial: Essays on Design and Design Studies*, design historian Victor Margolin (2002) provides a retrospective of design and design studies at the end of the millennium. By playing on the title of *The Sciences of the Artificial*, Margolin directly challenges Simon's "implicit assumption that one can devise plans of action without engaging with all the complexities and contradictions of the social world and without a critical reflection on those complexities" (2002: 7). More than simply a play on the title, Margolin devotes considerable attention to Simon in several of his essays, particularly in the ways in which the concept of "the artificial" and its relation to "the natural" has unfolded through new technologies and what he calls "technorhetoric."

Margolin captures the issues, concerns, and themes within the field of design as his personal concepts and interests continued to evolve over the final decades of the twentieth century. In the "Introduction" to *The Politics of the Artificial*, he writes about how his early quest "to explain the unifying principles that link all forms of knowledge no matter how seemingly disparate they were" would later evolve into thinking about design "as a vehicle that revealed human intentions for making the world" (2002: 2). During his career as a design historian and as a founder and editor of the journal *Design Issues* (published by MIT Press, 1984 to present) Margolin began to perceive designed objects "as evidence of a larger vision of how their designers thought the world was or might be." Envisioning design as seeing "how the world was or might be," Margolin argues that design exists in both of Simon's categories. In other words, in terms of Simon's concepts of the natural and artificial, he implies that design is both a science of the natural (how the world is and how it works) and the artificial (how the world might be). Margolin explains his concept of the "responsive environment," which he began to explore in 1984 and through which he attempted "to work out the problematic of how design might play a spiritual role in human development" (2002: 3). His interest in spirituality, an underlying value in his vision of sustainability, continues as a theme in his subsequent writings.

The importance of intradisciplinary discourse that would advance design as a self-reflective discipline and critical practice is an ongoing theme in Margolin's writing. Interdisciplinary communication that would facilitate cross-disciplinary knowledge flows and enable practitioners to join in pluridisciplinary collaboration is also one of his primary concerns. Margolin believed designers were lacking in their ability to communicate even amongst themselves, explaining that along with the division of training into professional specialties, such as architecture (which "remains at the apex of design hierarchy"), graphic design, product, and industrial design, "practitioners in these specialties place differing values on the importance of explaining to themselves and to others what they do" (2002: 29). He notes that product design, in particular, has been slow to adopt self-reflection. Citing European design as an example, Margolin argues that product design, being narrowly defined "as a practice of shaping material objects," was rooted in fine arts. Only over time did the practice adopt a "limited body of technical knowledge" (2002: 30).

A similar situation existed in the United States in the 1930s. The acceptance of design as a component of the manufacturing process coincided with the emergence of designers including Raymond Loewy (1893–1986), Walter Dorwin Teague (1883–1960), Norman Bel Geddes (1892–1958), and Henry Dreyfuss (1904–1972), whose sleek, modernist designs have become iconic. In transportation, for example,

Loewy is known for the design of the Pennsylvania Railroad S1 steam locomotive, designs for car manufacturer, Studebaker, and interiors for the Concorde and NASA's Skylab. Loewy's designs, the futuristic projects of Bel Geddes, and telecommunications products such as the Western Electric 302 telephone and the Princess phone designed by Henry Dreyfuss firmly established midcentury modernist design. Logos designed by Loewy for industrial giants, including Exxon, Shell, BP, and TWA are considered classics. Margolin notes that these individuals came to design with backgrounds in illustration, stage design, or related areas of practice. In his opinion, they were "opportunists and showmen," hiring staff that were versed in the necessary technical skills, such as drafting and engineering. As a group, Margolin claims that they "were known for their artistic knowledge rather than their technical expertise." He notes that Henry Dreyfuss was an exception due to his adoption of human factors into the design process. They pioneered a way of designing known as *styling*, "giving the product a strong visual image" (2002: 30). They were able to deliver a consistent method and presentation that inspired confidence in their clients.

Unraveling the Politics: A Critique of the Artificial

The central theme addressed in Margolin's essay *The Politics of the Artificial* is "the artificial and its boundaries" (2002: 109). Margolin uses Simon's positioning of design as a "science of the artificial" – the man-made and intentionally transformative – as a starting point for an ambitious overview of postmodern intellectual movements. This essay is important in that it highlights the postmodern influence and implications for design and for the limits of Simon's notion of "the artificial."

Margolin begins by reminding us that until relatively recently, the distinction between "nature and culture," or the natural and the artificial, was clear, "with design, of course, belonging to the realm of the culture" (2002: 107).

> If we consider design to be the conception and planning of the artificial, then its scope and boundaries are intimately entwined with our understanding of the artificial's limits. That is to say, extending the domain within which we conceive and plan, we are extending the boundaries of design practice. To the degree that design makes incursions into the realms that were once considered as belonging to nature rather than culture, so does its conceptual scope widen.
>
> *(2002: 107)*

To put this statement in perspective, it is necessary to recall the shift that began in the mid-twentieth century from the object to the user. Margolin notes that for early design theorists, such as Henry Cole,[8] the concept of design was "inextricably bound to the object" with the role of the designer being "to improve the appearance of products."

This discourse and the relationship it forged between design and industry continues well into present times. The emphasis on _styling,_ a term that most contemporary designers eschew as grossly limiting their capabilities, was unabashedly evident in the "American consultant designers" of the 1930s that were discussed previously.

Until recently the focus on the object defined professional design. In parallel, theorists including Herbert Simon and John Chris Jones began to extend the concept of design more broadly, arguing that _a design process_ "underlies everything in our culture, both material and immaterial" (Margolin, 2002: 108). Simon would proclaim that "Everyone designs who devises courses of action aimed at changing existing situations into preferred ones" (1996: 111).

Assuming Simon's position that design exists in the realm of the artificial, Margolin frames his discussion of design theorists and the intellectual movements they represented around two terms that became contested in the world of the postmodern: _meaning_ and _reality_. Questions that were raised about meaning – the meaning of objects and of design – and about the nature of reality in the contemporary world, signaled that the boundary between nature and the artificial was becoming blurred. Beginning with the modernist movement, Margolin traces the discourse of early modernist designers who "believed that meaning was embedded in the object rather than negotiated in the relation between object and user."

> Objects were considered to be signs of value with uncontested referents such as clarity, beauty, integrity, simplicity, economy of means, and function. The reductive slogan 'form follows function' assumed that use was an explicit, unambiguous term. Thus the meaning of objects was found in their relation to a value that was grounded in belief.
>
> _(2002: 108)_

The idea of "grounded belief" and the conditions under which the "right" to assign meaning was exercised, were challenged by the poststructuralists. Yet a more difficult problem was raised regarding _the nature of reality_, which, according to Margolin, was uncontested by the early modernists. He cites Andrea Branzi's (1988) recognition that there were, in fact, two modernities,

> For the first modernity…reality was an uncontested term. It was considered stable ground for the attribution of meaning to objects, images, and acts. Today, this is no longer the case, and any mention of 'reality' must be qualified by conditions, just as the use of the term 'meaning' must be; hence we are unclear as to how or whether boundaries can be drawn around the real or authentic as a basis of meaning.
>
> _(2002: 108)_

Margolin argues that in retrospect, Simon's 1969 call for a "science of the artificial" cast nature in a supporting role "as a ground of meaning against which such a science or a broadly conceived practice of design would be defined" (2002: 109). Although the sharp distinction between natural and artificial and broad generalization of their roles were clear to Simon, the second wave of modernity that Branzi identified cast this certainty into question.

Margolin asserts that Simon's "positivist construction of the natural was also the model for his explicit methodology of design" (2002: 108–109). For Simon, the natural and artificial sciences rest on *different* forms of logic – declarative logic for the natural sciences and a "modest adaptation of ordinary declarative logic" (Simon, 1996: 115) for the sciences of the artificial. However, Margolin argues, the methods used to do artificial science were modeled after those required for the natural sciences. Simon's glossing over of methodological differences, *the ways of doing*, is out of line with his sharp distinction in the construction of *ways of knowing* between the natural and artificial sciences.

The transition between Branzi's first and second modernities is not seamless on any dimension, whether psychologically, temporally, virtually, or geographically. Subsequent intellectual movements and critiques of the postmodern have shifted the horizon beyond Branzi's two modernities. Collectively we are living in multiple modernities at once.

Scientific "Truth": Blurring the Boundaries of Natural and Artificial

By focusing on scientific thought as a linguistic construct, critics have attempted to challenge a previous faith in scientific truth. Hence, we have two contested terms, 'meaning' and 'reality', that severely undermine the certainties on which a theory and practice of design was built in the first modernity.

(Margolin, 2002: 109)

Critiques of the postmodern period raised more questions concerning the validity of both meaning and reality, challenging the "easy equation of the natural with the real." Margolin notes Paul Feyerabend (1988), Donna Haraway (1994), Stanley Aronowitz (1988), Jean-François Lyotard (1984), and many others who chipped away at the belief in scientific and objective truth. Calling into question claims to know nature as real, these critiques problematized equating nature and the natural with what is real (2002: 109). With these terms in question, design discourse would need to change, thus challenging Simon's classification of natural and artificial sciences. Although Margolin was unclear about how a new discourse would develop "as a reflection of design practice," he believed that the central theme would be "the artificial and its boundaries" (2002: 109).

Margolin notes that Simon delivered the first Compton Lectures in 1969 at MIT, to a primarily technology-oriented audience with a propensity toward invention and most likely receptive to his characterization of design. Simon's distinction between the natural and artificial "marked the task of humans to invent the artificial world in order to achieve their own goals while honoring the parallel purpose of the natural world" (2002: 109). Thus, the artificial is the result of human agency that involves synthesis and the act of making: the domain of design. According to Simon, one of the distinguishing characteristics of the artificial is that "Artificial things may imitate appearances in natural things, while lacking, in one or many respects, *the reality of the latter* [italics added]" (1996: 5). The natural world is to be observed, described, and analyzed whereas the artificial world, a product of design and invention, can imitate the natural world, but never be commensurable with it. In Simon's view, the artificial and the natural are clearly bounded and incommensurable.

The postmodernist challenge to the implicit assumption that equates nature with reality problematizes the boundaries of Simon's distinction between the natural and artificial. Margolin argues that blurring the boundaries combined with the technical possibilities of rapidly advancing fields such as biotechnology create the possibility that rather than an *imitation* of nature, the artificial becomes a *replacement* for it (2002: 112).

Contemporary Critiques of Design

What are the implications of the postmodern critique for design? How might we reconcile Simon's broad definition of design that includes not only the traditional professional fields of industrial and product design, graphic design, and architecture, but also the emerging fields of service design, interaction and experience design, as well as technology design and hybrid disciplines such as biotechnology? Is it possible to detach the products of design in any of these fields from their social and cultural contexts or from their intended and unintended consequences?

Margolin argues that despite their ability to design successful products, with only a few notable exceptions,[9] the legacy of most twentieth century designers did not include attention to "the cultural or social issues of their profession" (2002: 30). Divisions within design about the value assigned to technical and aesthetic knowledge contributed to the lack of reflection and "critical theory of practice" (2002: 37). Victor Papanek (1973) and others who raised issues about the social and cultural conditions in which product or industrial design is practiced, were unable during their lifetimes to elevate this discourse to a level that permeated the entire field and served as a vehicle for continual self-reflection and debate. However, their contributions continued to reverberate through following decades, providing a commentary on issues that included sustainability, the commercialization of design, and its relationship to industry and technoscience.

Although a minority, there were, in fact, many designers in the postwar period that were critical of professional design's lack of attention to the social, cultural, and environmental impact of its practices. In the opening keynote of the Design Anthropology Futures conference, Alison Clarke (2015) identified the 1960s and 1970s as the beginnings of design anthropology, noting a shift away from the practice of "industrial making" represented by the Ulm school toward the anthropological and contextual. Clarke described the challenge of Papanek

and others to the dominant commercial design paradigm citing the Italian d\
journal *Casabella* that promoted design as an interdisciplinary field and Ern\
Rogers' editorial "Continuity" (1954), also known as the *Casabella* manifes\
that rejected the concept of design as an inducement to consume.

Critiques of design from both within and outside the field have been docu-mented by many theorists and practitioners that were deeply immersed in the field. This recounting covers only a very few. However, is important to note that critiques continued beyond the postwar period and into the present as the visibility of design has increased in the media, as designers have been tasked with solving more complex problems, and as design in contemporary culture has become nearly synonymous with innovation, future-making, and technological advancement. For example, the assertion by a Silicon Valley technologist that "The future arrives here sooner" provoked a response from anthropologist Lucy Suchman as she observed that the character of a technological society is reflected in how innovation is inextricably linked to technological advance.

> One of the marks of a technological society, Barry (2001) observes, is an orientation that privileges change and then figures change as technological innovation (p. 201). Innovation, in turn, is embedded within a broader cultural imaginary that posits a world that is always lagging, always in need of being brought up to date through the intercessions of those trained to shape it: a world, in sum, in need of design.
>
> *(2011: 5)*

When the power and impact of professional design is harnessed to the design of technology in a way that is not self-reflective and critical of its own practices, the outcomes for society, culture, and the environment will be at best a tertiary concern. Changing perspectives within design and a growing sense of account-ability among designers for their role as contributors to the "wicked problems" (Buchanan, 1992; Rittel & Webber, 1973, 1984) that they are now called to solve have emerged in the field and in design education.

The Social Turn: Design for the Other 90%

Media coverage of design's success in product development has generated unbri-dled enthusiasm for "design thinking" as an alternative approach to solving crit-ical social problems. The Cooper-Hewitt National Design Museum exhibition, *Design for the Other 90%* (Smithsonian, 2007), featured a selection of examples that represented a movement of "designers, engineers, students and professors, architects, and social entrepreneurs" from around the world that addressed the needs of underserved populations,

> This movement has its roots in the 1960s and 1970s, when economists and designers looked to find simple, low-cost solutions to combat poverty. More

recently, designers are working directly with end users of their products, emphasizing co-creation to respond to their needs. Many of these projects employ market principles for income generation as a way out of poverty. Poor rural farmers become micro-entrepreneurs, while cottage industries emerge in more urban areas. Some designs are patented to control the quality of their important breakthroughs, while others are open source in nature to allow for easier dissemination and adaptation, locally and internationally.

(Smithsonian, 2007)

Marking a turn to innovation in the social realm, the movement is characterized as

Encompassing a broad set of modern social and economic concerns, these design innovations often support responsible, sustainable economic policy. They help, rather than exploit, poorer economies; minimize environmental impact; increase social inclusion; improve healthcare at all levels; and advance the quality and accessibility of education. These designers' voices are passionate, and their points of view range widely on how best to address these important issues. Each object on display tells a story, and provides a window through which we can observe this expanding field. *Design for the Other 90%* demonstrates how design can be a dynamic force in saving and transforming lives, at home and around the world.

(Smithsonian, 2007)

As social innovation opened a pathway for designers of conscience, a new wave of critique ensued.

Is Humanitarian Design the New Imperialism?

As media coverage raised awareness among the general public of design's expanding role, questions have been raised as to the suitability of design, and the skill sets and education of designers to take on the kinds of social innovation that were featured in *Design for the Other 90%*. Asking whether "humanitarian design" was "the new imperialism" (Nussbaum, 2010), design critic Bruce Nussbaum described how his enthusiasm for the call for designers to "do good" and "change the world" was clouded by the less than enthusiastic responses of non-Western audience participants. Nussbaum witnessed that at two different presentations, non-Westerners took offense at the assumptions underlying high visibility design artifacts like One Laptop per Child and the XO Tablet (OLPC, 2015). Reflecting on the difference between responses from the European and American audience members and those of the non-Westerners in the audience following a presentation by designer Emily Pilliton (Studio H), Nussbaum recalled that

Of course there was polite applause but, to my surprise, there was also a lot of loud grumbling against Emily along the lines of "What makes her think she can just come in and solve *our* problems?" This was a challenge of presumption that just stopped me cold—and sent me back to my Peace Corps days when I heard a lot about Western cultural imperialism from my Filipino friends...Are designers the new anthropologists or missionaries, come to poke into village life, "understand" it and make it better—their "modern" way?

(Nussbaum, 2010)

Nussbaum is not alone in raising these concerns. Echoing earlier calls for "decolonization," anthropologist Elizabeth (Dori) Tunstall (2013) proposed "the methodology of design anthropology as an answer to how one might create decolonized processes of design and anthropological engagement" (2013: 232). Like Nussbaum, Tunstall questioned the assumptions of applying design thinking to solve humanitarian problems: "While design thinking represents an advance in Western business thought, what does it mean to bring design thinking to places that already have their own indigenous forms of thinking also critical of linear and rational models?" (2013: 237).

Having adopted a critical stance toward its legacy as "handmaiden to colonialism," anthropology is in a position to inform the design process in ways that problematize the role of design innovation while calling attention to indigenous ways of knowing. Citing Faye Harrison (2010), Tunstall advocates for "design anthropology that frees its parent fields from 'the prevailing forces of global inequality and dehumanization and to locate it firmly in the complex struggle for genuine transformation'" (2013: 245). Arguing for design anthropology as a "decolonized methodology" Tunstall concludes that

> Design innovation and anthropology have much that they can contribute to fighting global inequality, but first it should adhere to clear principles of respectful engagement with people's values, the translation of them through processes of inclusive codesign, and the evaluation of their effects on people's experiences from the perspective of the most vulnerable.
>
> *(2013: 245)*

At this point it is worth noting that new avenues of design practice entail extensive experimentation which, as these critiques reveal, necessarily results in failures, mistakes, and wrong turns. Yet each new exploration embodies renewed hope in design as a vehicle for improving life on the planet, not only for an elite fortunate few, but for a sustainable future for all human and nonhuman life.

Branzi's Dilemma: Design Consciousness in Contemporary Culture

Many of the conversations that shaped the development of design over the last decades of the twentieth century occurred across continents between design practitioners and theorists. Perhaps even more than they do today, design journals, conferences, and seminars served as important forums for the exchange of ideas and for debates about the role of design in contemporary society and culture. Often, as in the following nple, articles were published and republished in various formats as a way of introducing, reintroducing, or supporting particular points of view. This provided direction and content for ongoing conversations, debate, and discourse. One of these conversations was sparked by the journal article "We Are the Primitives" (Branzi, 1986) which was originally published in 1985 in the Italian journal, *Modo*. Written by Italian designer, educator, and author, Andrea Branzi, the article became the focal point in Richard Buchanan's 1994 keynote address presented at an international conference held at the University of Art and Design in Helsinki.[10]

Buchanan's keynote, which was later published in the journal *Design Issues* (Buchanan, 1998), addressed the conference theme "Design: Pleasure or Responsibility" by highlighting a dilemma faced by individuals and groups "in the new circumstances of contemporary culture: how to find identity and moral purpose when central values are *essentially contested*" (1998: 3). The article was selected not because Buchanan agreed with Branzi, but rather because he believed that Branzi stated this challenge "with clarity and elegance." Buchanan noted that the conference itself with its theme indicating the choice of either pleasure or responsibility was a sign of the changes that had impacted design over the previous decades and that were continuing to unfold.

According to Buchanan, the challenge of finding "identity and moral purpose" rested on a deeper dilemma: the fate of design was not determined entirely within framework of design culture or by few individuals, but instead "lies within the framework of culture as a whole." (1998: 3)

> This framework is changing before our eyes, altering the attitudes of public, the environment of corporations, and the way we understand all the professions with which we much collaborate in developing new products.
>
> *(1998: 3–4)*

The concern is not with the "surface of culture" – the continuously changing fads, styles, and trends. Instead, Buchanan is referring to the "philosophic engine that stands behind the cultural: the fundamental issues, problems, and ideas that are shared with varying degrees of understanding by all participants" (Buchanan, 1998: 4). By situating design culture within the framework of culture as a whole, Buchanan aligns himself with Branzi's concept of the "neoprimitive condition," which "is not a design in the sense that it does not wish to be the latest trend of the avant-garde fashion; but it is precisely a condition into which various languages and already diffuse attitudes fuse" (1986: 23).

The philosophic engine that Buchanan referred to "is what Branzi perceives in his essay, and his perception is strengthened precisely because he is uncomfortable with the form that this new engine has taken."

> ...he believes, at least in principle, that the cultural and philosophic revolution that began in the early decades of the twentieth century has taken another turn and continues to move forward with unabated force to the present.
>
> *(Buchanan, 1998: 4)*

The essence of "Branzi's dilemma," according to Buchanan, was widely recognized in the last decades of the twentieth century. Often referred to as the
"collapse of modernism," the dilemma stems from a loss of faith in the ideals
of modernism and its failure to maintain a "unifying ideology of design and
culture." The promise of modernism as a means to an improved and even
perfected humanity through progress in art, design, and technology failed
to deliver. Buchanan agreed with Branzi that "the 'ideological parachute' of
modernism no longer works" (1986: 4). While postmodernism illustrated the
fault lines of modernism, as an intellectual movement it did little to offer inspiration and offered even less in defining a unifying alternative to modernist
ideology.

The dilemma that Buchanan described rested on a question and a search for
alternatives: "if there is no unifying ideology shared by the design community
and world culture as a whole, where does the individual find identity and moral
purpose?" (Buchanan, 1998: 5). He rejects Branzi's alternative that it is up to
individuals to find meaning in their personal identity.

> that without a unifying ideology in the culture around us, each individual
> must look within himself or herself for the original key – the language and
> code – of personal identity. There is no longer world culture; there are
> only individuals, each grappling to make personal order and sense out of
> an increasingly complex world.
>
> *(Buchanan, 1998: 6)*

Offering an alternative, Buchanan identified four main approaches that helped to
shape design and the profession of design in the twentieth century. He characterizes the two-term either/or of the dilemma between modernist and postmodernist theory as "impoverished" and suggests instead that

> ...if we are correct in identifying deliberation and dialogue – dialogue as
> a new form of rhetoric and dialectic in community activity – as central
> themes in the new circumstances of the contemporary world, then a third
> alternative also exists, representing a more supple three-term dialectic
> suited to the needs of our complex situation. This third term is the medi-
> ated middle in any good discussion. It is the domain, not of dogmatically
> asserted truth on either side of an issue, but of honest uncertainty, hypoth-
> esis, and possibility. It is the domain of cooperation in common enterprise,
> despite differences of personal values or ideologies.
>
> *(Buchanan, 1998: 17)*

Buchanan's proposal to resolve Branzi's dilemma is deceptively simple: a collective solution to resolve "the two-term either/or of the dilemma between
modernist and postmodernist theory," an alternative to cynicism and nar-
cissism, and a path to finding identity and moral purpose. He concludes by
stating

There is one observation that has immediate bearing on the work of designers today. If the arguments we have advanced are valid and useful, the task is no longer to design for a universal audience, or national groups, or market segments, or even the ideological abstraction known as "the consumer." Despite the continuing role of mass-production in many societies, the task is to design for the *individual placed in his or her immediate context*. Our products should support the individual in the effort to become an active participant in culture, searching for locally significant coherence and connection. Products should be personal pathways in the otherwise confusing ecology of culture.

(Buchanan, 1998: 20)

How is this task to be accomplished? Buchanan does not leave off with a call to "Just do it." Acknowledging the difficulty of this challenge, he also addressed the ways in which designers are better prepared for the task through advances in design education that advocate for increased sensitivity to individuals as well as to how different kinds of knowledge bear on design. Recognizing that we might find some of the design we see distressing, but we will be delighted by other work, he concludes by reminding us that we are engaged in an experiment.

Design is very young and has far to go in the exploration of its role in culture. For many of us, this means better understanding of the disciplines of design thinking, not merely changes in style and surface treatment. Our hope is that the quality of discussion about design continues to improve and that designers do not become afraid of having their ideas and work subjected to wider and more insightful discussion than in the past. We all have much to learn about living together in a culture that is not fixed and changeless, and this is both our pleasure and our responsibility.

(Buchanan, 1998: 20)

Twenty-First Century Design: An Integrative Discipline

In modern societies with their emphasis on innovation and change, which are often considered as intrinsic values (Suchman, 2011) design has arguably become one of the major sites of cultural production and change, on par with science, technology, and art.

(Otto & Smith, 2013: 2)

The final sections in this exploration of design anthropology's design roots cover a series of texts that signaled the changing scope and perceptions of design from within and outside the field. Although each highlights a different aspect of design as a group, they address developments that led to the recognition of design as an *integrative discipline* (Buchanan, 1992: 14), and facilitated the confluence of design and anthropology.

The Design Education Manifesto

In 2011, designer and design thought leader, Hugh Dubberly, provided input to an update of the International Council of Graphic Design Associations (ICOGDA) "Design Education Manifesto." First published in 2000, the Manifesto anticipated the new challenges and contexts that reflected shifts in technology, economic structure, and culture. Dubberly predicted that

> In the new world of information and biology, design will change. Less common will be situations in which things are designed by designers, in advance of use by users, enforcing a single view. More common will be situations created by participants, during use, enabling multiple views. Today's users will become designers; today's designers will become meta-designers, creating conditions in which others can design.
>
> *(2011: 2)*

Summarizing his remarks Dubberly (2011) issued this warning,

> The design practice that grew out of the industrial revolution is no longer sustainable (economically or ecologically). A new practice – one that responds to the information revolution – has begun to emerge. We can see its outlines, but much remains to be invented. For this, we must take responsibility. In addition, we must invent a mechanism (an organic system) through which the discipline of design can learn and evolve.
>
> At the same time, design education still largely reflects design's origins in craftwork. Simply put: Design education is out of date. What is worse: Change is accelerating, and design education is stuck. It has little means to move forward. We must also take responsibility for re-inventing design education and integrating it into an organic system through which the discipline of design evolves.
>
> *(2011: 3)*

Manifestos signal important shifts in thinking. However, the true test of their significance is what happens over time as the passion subsides. Will the fervor and commitment to a new set of values transfer to action on the ground? Institutional change[11] is slow. Cultural transformation is a complex process that is dependent on many factors. Some of these, like leadership and structure, are internal. Other factors, like economic, political, and market forces are external and have varying degrees of influence. Culture is manifest in various ways, both symbolic and material. However, core values underpin all cultural manifestations.

Rhetoric can be an early indicator signaling the intention to change. It is relatively easy to shift rhetoric. Some of the material trappings of culture are also comparatively easy to change, although they will likely be met with confusion and even resistance as they are incongruous with what people expect. Much more intensive effort is required to bring about deep cultural change within an institution because the core values that animate symbolic and material culture are carried in the hearts and minds of individual people.

And yet institutional change does occur. Design education in the second decade of the twentieth century is not what it was a generation ago. It is rare to find a design curriculum that does not include some form of training in human-centered methods. New technologies are being integrated into all phases of the design process and exist side-by-side with stock and trade artifacts like Post-It Notes, whiteboards, and Sharpies. Like Branzi's modernities, we are simultaneously navigating past and present while designing the future.

Designing With, Not Designing For: Participatory Design and Co-creation

The aim of Chapters 1 and 2 is to draw together threads of discourse and to describe the conditions that over time prepared the ground for design anthropology to emerge as a transdisciplinary field of praxis. The participatory design movement, emerging from Scandinavian workplace studies of the 1960s and 1970s, signaled a major development in the evolution of contemporary design. As a group, these studies introduced design and social science methods, opening a pathway for an integrated design practice by "challenging the use of technology and the management prerogative to define what may count as innovation" (Ehn, Nilsson, & Topgaard, 2014: 7).

Participatory design is an approach motivated by values that support local knowledge production and active inclusion in designing solutions that seek to ensure usability and to satisfy the needs of all stakeholders. As in other forms of design practice, participatory design is grounded in invention and the innovation process. However, it differs in that actual and potential users are invited to participate in phases of problem identification, solution-finding, and prototype testing. In practice, the participatory design process involves a broad range of stakeholders in addressing issues of place, social and technical appropriateness, politics and power, and cultural fit. It reflects a paradigm shift that has influenced design practice, design discourse, and design education across the world, and has found expression in terms such as democratizing design, cocreation, collaborative prototyping, social design, and user-driven and consumer-driven innovation (Ehn & Lowgren, 1996; Hippel, 2005; Prahalad & Krishnan, 2008; Hippel, Ogawa, & Jong, 2011; Ehn, Nilsson, & Topgaard, 2014).

Participatory design has become a well-documented form of design practiced in numerous fields from software and product development to health care, community planning, and placemaking. In recognition of the potential of customers and users as a source of innovation, participatory design methods have been adopted in business and industry. Today the influence of participatory design can be seen in virtual platforms that facilitate crowdsourcing as a form of user-centered and open-source innovation.

Ethnography in the Field of Design

> History is our collective experience. The more we know of it, the more
> we can use it to question the prevailing values of society. To be without a
> knowledge of history is to give up a space outside the system where one can
> find alternatives and also empowerment for change.
>
> *(Margolin, 2002: 241)*

While Participatory Design (PD) was shaping European and Scandinavian design, in the United States a growing awareness of the social induced a shift from
object-centered to human-centered design creating the conditions for the introduction of ethnographic approaches in business and industry. In the article
Ethnography in the Field of Design, mentioned in the previous chapter, Wasson
(2000) notes that anthropologists had been studying issues of consumption
(Douglas & Sherwood, 1979), gifts and economic exchange (Mauss, 1990;
Malinowski, 1961), and popular culture years before the field of design "discovered" ethnography.

> Since at least the 1980s, applied anthropologists have consulted on mar-
> keting and product development in the private sector (Baba 1986; Barnett
> 1992; Sherry 1995). But these anthropologists were not integrated into
> the design community. Their recommendations to corporate clients were
> summaries of research findings; translating these findings into concrete
> products was left to the clients.
>
> *(Wasson, 2000: 379)*

The inclusion of anthropologists as active participants alongside designers advanced relatively rapidly in the United States. It has been driven by the in-
novation/collaboration paradigm and deployment of pluridisciplinary teams
in business and industry, pioneered by anthropologists in the field of software
development. Wasson describes how anthropologists were "prominent members" in the Computer-Supported Cooperative Work (CSCW) community
where their contributions highlighted "the importance of empirically examining
the everyday practices of computer users." Similar efforts to expand the focus of
design research were made by other social scientists.

> Prior to the link with anthropology, in the 1980s and early 1990s, sev-
> eral researchers working in the field of design had already initiated stud-
> ies showing the importance of situating product use in its sociocultural
> contexts. The work of these individuals undoubtedly created a more re-
> ceptive environment for the subsequent wave of ethnographic research.
> Two researchers who became particularly well known – and are still highly
> respected – were Fulton Suri at IDEO and Liz Sanders of Sonic Rim.
>
> *(Wasson, 2000: 380)*

The critiques of the postwar period and the social turn that was signaled by the increasing focus on "the user" as a "central trope for designers" (Wasson, 2000: 377) created the conditions for the diffusion of ethnography and the adaptation of ethnographic methods in design research. Wasson notes that before the introduction of ethnography, cognitive psychology and human factors were the dominant lenses used to understand users, and to study product usability rather than the relationships between the object and the user.

> To give a simple example, how do we know whether to push or pull a door to open it? Some doors are confusing in this regard, but their hardware can be designed to make the answer clear…In this approach to 'usability,' research is largely restricted to a consideration of what goes on 'in the head' of the user. The way the product use is embedded in larger institutional and cultural contexts is not extensively examined (Robinson, 1993).
>
> *(2000: 377–378)*

Designers also used market research in the form of customer surveys, customer demographics, and purchasing patterns over time that "identify large-scale statistical patterns, but offered little detail about how product use fits into consumers' everyday practices" (Wasson, 2000: 378).

Although designers continue to use the term "ethnography," there is often no recognition of where the ethnographic method originated or an understanding of why and how it came to be adopted in the field. The recontextualization of ethnography in design has raised questions about the ethics of how designers use ethnographic methods (Miller, 2014), about what ethnography means in the context of design, and whether the form of ethnography that is practiced by designers qualifies as ethnography by anthropological standards. Wasson argues that

> 'Ethnography' has a narrower and somewhat different meaning in the field of design than it does for most anthropologists. In common with other kinds of applied anthropology, research is usually done more quickly and given less theoretical contextualization, than on academic projects. In addition, however, the data collection methods and ways ethnographic materials are analyzed are shaped by the particular needs of industrial designers. They are also molded by the traditions of CSCW ethnography.
>
> *(2000: 382)*

There is no question that designers are practicing a different form of ethnography from what anthropologists consider qualifies as ethnographic research. The differences involve the process of translation, repurposing, and recontextualization of ethnography from anthropology to design. For example, Wasson notes that ethnography in design is associated more with data collection than with data analysis (2000, 383). However, this is understandable given that the goals of ethnographic research in design are very different from the goals of anthropological research, which might be an ethnographic monograph. According to Wasson

> The goal of data analysis was to develop a model that both interpreted the ethnographic materials that had been collected and envisioned a solution for the client. The model offered a coherent narrative about the world of user-product interactions: how a product was incorporated into consumers' daily routines and what symbolic meanings it held for them. These insights, in turn, were framed to have clear implications for the client's product development and marketing efforts.
>
> *(2000: 384)*

The widespread attention that design has received in the popular business press since the 1990s has coincided with the diffusion and adaptation of ethnographic methods within design practice and the changing role of design within business. As noted in the previous section, the proliferation of enthusiastic media coverage has raised concerns about whether design and designers are equipped to take on the challenges they are being tasked to solve. Writing at the beginning of the new millennium, Wasson cautioned that despite the popularity of ethnography within design, factors including client confidentiality and the time involved in product development, "it is impossible to know precisely what contributions ethnography has made in the field of design" (2000: 384).

We know today that ethnography in design *has* stood the test of time and is now embedded in design education under the rubric of design research and "contextual research" (Holtzblatt & Beyer, 2014). From an anthropological perspective, the contention that ethnography in design has become a "pale shadow of itself" (Wasson, 2000, 2002) is widely accepted. This is not surprising since historically, the purpose, goals, and objectives of the two fields have been vastly different. The tasks now revolve around finding a path from pluridisciplinarity to transdisciplinarity, a path that is being forged by design anthropologists.

This chapter has presented a case for how it came to be that designers needed a method that enabled a deeper understanding of humans and the social realm – in other words, ethnography – in order to solve the problems with which they were confronted. External conditions and internal circumstances within each field have aligned to create opportunities for designers and anthropologists to work together. The work that has resulted from the confluence of design and anthropology is the focus of the chapters that follow.

Notes

1 https://en.wikipedia.org/wiki/Utility.
2 In 1947, the Herman Miller Company of Zeeland, Michigan, known as one of the premier design firms, began production of the Eames chair, which it continues to manufacture today.

3 Wright's use of reinforced concrete in the design of Unity Temple (Oak Park, IL 1905–1909) which is said to have been the first "modern building."
4 Perhaps the most recognized example is Fallingwater in Mill Run, Pennsylvania (1937).
5 https://en.wikipedia.org/wiki/Frank_Lloyd_Wright.
6 www.hfg-archiv.ulm.de/english/.
7 Bauhaus (1919–1933) is described as "the first academy for design in the world." It was a response to the Industrial Revolution and dehumanization, an attempt to keep art and craft from being lost to mass production. http://bauhaus-online.de/en.
8 Henry Cole is mentioned as being a chief promoter of Britain's Crystal Palace Exhibition in 1851. Margolin notes that Cole was a proponent of close collaboration between "artists and industry" (Margolin, 2002: 107).
9 These exceptions include the influence of William Morris (1834–1896) and the Arts and Crafts movement of the late nineteenth century, and Frank Lloyd Wright's (1867–1959) philosophy of organic architecture.
10 "We Are the Primitives" was later included in *Design Discourse: History, Theory, Criticism* (Margolin, 1989).
11 In this context, institutional change implies disciplinary as well as organizational change.

References

Aronowitz, Stanley. 1988. *Science as Power: Discourse and Ideology in Modern Society.* Minneapolis: University of Minnesota Press.

Baba, Marietta. 1986. *Business and Industrial Anthropology: An Overview.* NAPA Bulletin No. 2. Washington, DC: National Association for the Practice of Anthropology.

Barnett, Steven. 1992. *The Nissan Report.* New York: Doubleday.

Barry, Andrew. 2001. *Political Machines: Governing a Technological Society.* London: Athlone.

Branzi, Andrea. 1986. We Are the Primitives. *Design Issues*, 3(1), 23–27.

———. 1988. *Leaning from Milan: Design and the Second Modernity.* Cambridge, MA: MIT Press.

Buchanan, Richard. 1992. Wicked Problems in Design Thinking. *Design Issues*, 8(2), 5–21.

———. 1998. Branzi's Dilemma: Design in Contemporary Culture. *Design Issues*, 14(1), 3–20.

Clarke, Alison J. 2015. *The New Ethnographers: Design Activism 1968–1974.* Paper Presented at the Design Anthropological Futures Conference, Copenhagen, Denmark.

Douglas, Mary and Baron Sherwood. 1979. *The World of Goods: Towards an Anthropology of Consumption.* New York: Routledge.

Dubberly, Hugh. 2011. Input for Updating the ICOGRADA Design Education Manifesto. *ICOGRADA Design Education Manifesto*, 76–81.

Ehn, Pelle and Jonas Lowgren. 1996. The Qualiteque: Systems at an Exhibition. Interactions, 3(3), 53–55.

Ehn, Pelle, Elisabet M. Nilsson, and Richard Topgaard. 2014. Introduction. In P. Ehn, E.M. Nilsson, and R. Topgaard (Eds.), *Making Futures: Marginal Notes on Innovation, Design, and Democracy*, 1–13. Cambridge, MA: MIT Press.

Feyerabend, Paul. 1988. *Farewell to Reason.* New York: Verso.

Forsythe, Diane. 1999. "It's Just a Matter of Common Sense": Ethnography as Invisible Work. *Computer Supported Cooperative Work*, 8, 127–145.

Gatt, Caroline and Tim Ingold. 2013. From Description to Correspondence. In W. Gunn, T. Otto, and R. Smith (Eds.), *Design Anthropology: Theory and Practice*, 139–158. New York: Bloomsbury.

Gigerenzer, Gerd and Reinhard Selten (Eds.). 2002. *Bounded Rationality: The Adaptive Toolbox*. Cambridge, MA: MIT Press.

Haraway, Donna. 1994. A Manifesto for Cyborgs: Science, Technology, and Socialist Feminism in the 1980s. In S. Seidman (Ed.), *The Postmodern Turn: New Perspectives on Social Theory*, 82–115. Cambridge, UK: Cambridge University Press.

Harrison, Faye V. 2010. Anthropology as an Agent of Transformation. In F. Harrison (Ed.), *Decolonizing Anthropology: Moving Further Toward an Anthropology of Liberation*, 1–14. Arlington, VA: American Anthropological Association.

Hippel, Eric von. 2005. *Democratizing Innovation*. Cambridge, MA: MIT Press.

Hippel, Eric von, Susumu Ogawa, and Jeroen P.J. De Jong. 2011. The Age of the Consumer-Innovator. *MIT Sloan Management Review*, 53(1), 27–35.

Holtzblatt, Katherine and Hugh Beyer. 2014. Contextual Design. In M. Soegaard and R.F. Dam (Eds.), *The Encyclopedia of Human-Computer Interaction* (2nd Ed.). Aarhus, Denmark: The Interaction Design Foundation.

Kjaersgaard, Mette G. 2013. (Trans)forming Knowledge and Design Concepts in the Design Workshop. In W. Gunn, T. Otto, and R.C. Smith (Eds.), *Design Anthropology: Theory and Practice*, 51–67. New York: Bloomsbury.

Lyotard, Jean-François. 1984. *The Postmodern Condition: A Report on Knowledge*. Trans. G. Bennington and B. Massumi. Minneapolis: University of Minnesota Press.

Malinowski, Bronislaw. 1961. *Argonauts of the Western Pacific: An Account of Native Enterprise and Adventure in the Archipelagoes of Melanesian New Guinea*. New York: E.P. Dutton. (Original edition was published in 1922.)

Marcuse, Herbert. 1964. *One Dimensional Man*. Boston: Beacon Press.

Margolin, Victor, Ed. 1989. *Design Discourse: History, Theory, Criticism*. Chicago: University of Chicago Press.

———2002. *The Politics of the Artificial: Essays on Design and Design Studies*. Chicago: University of Chicago Press.

Martin, Roger. 2009. *The Design of Business: Why Design Thinking Is the Next Competitive Advantage*. Brighton, MA: Harvard Business Press.

Mauss, Marcel. 1990. The Gift: The Form and Reason for Exchange in Archaic Societies. New York: W.W. Norton.

Miller, Christine. 2014. Lost in Translation? Ethics and Ethnography in Design Research. *Journal of Business Anthropology*, 4(1), 62–78.

Nussbaum, Bruce. 2010. Is Humanitarian Design the New Imperialism? *Fast Company, Design*. Retrieved from www.fastcodesign.com/1661859/is-humanitarian-design-the-new-imperialism.

One Laptop Per Child (OLPC). 2015. Introducing the XO Tablet. Retrieved from http://one.laptop.org/.

Papanek, Victor. 1973. Design for the Real World: Human Ecology and Social Change. New York: Bantam Books.

Peirce, Charles. 1877. The Fixation of Belief. *Popular Science Monthly*, 12, 1–15. Retrieved from www.pierce.org/writings/p107.html

Prahalad, C.K. and M.S. Krishnan. 2008. *The New Age of Innovation: Driving Co-Created Value through Global Networks*. New York: McGraw Hill.

Rittel, Horst and Melvin M. Webber. 1973. Dilemmas in General Theory of Planning. *Policy Sciences*, 4, 155–169.

———. 1984. Planning Problems are Wicked Problems. In N. Cross (Ed.), *Developments in Design Methodology*, 135–144. New York: John Wiley.

Robinson, Rick E. 1993. What to Do with a Human Factor: A Manifest of Sorts. *American Center for Design Journal*, 7, 63–73.

Rogers, Ernesto. 1954. Continuitá/Continuity. *Casabella*, 199, 2–3.

Sherry, John F., Jr. 1995. *Contemporary Marketing and Consumer Behavior: An Anthropological Sourcebook*. Thousand Oaks, CA: Sage.

Simon, Herbert. 1956. Rational Choice and the Structure of the Environment. *Psychological Review*, 63(2), 129–138.

———. 1969. *The Sciences of the Artificial*. Cambridge: MIT Press.

———. 1973. The Structure of Ill-structured Problems. *Artificial Intelligence*, 4, 181–201.

———. 1996. *The Sciences of the Artificial*. (3rd Ed.) Cambridge: MIT Press.

Smithsonian. 2007. *Design for the Other 90%*. Retrieved from http://archive.cooperhewitt.org/other90/other90.cooperhewitt.org/index.html

Star, Susan Leigh. 1989. *Regions of the Mind: Brain Research and the Quest for Scientific Certainty*. Stanford, CA: Stanford University Press.

Suchman, Lucy. 2011. Anthropological Relocations and the Limits of Design. *Annual Review of Anthropology*, 40, 1–18.

Tunstall, Elizabeth. 2013. Decolonizing Design Innovation: Design Anthropology, Critical Anthropology, and Indigenous Knowledge. In W. Gunn, T. Otto, and R.C. Smiths.), *Design Anthropology: Theory and Practice*, 232–250. New York: Bloomsbury.

Wasson, Christina. 2000. Ethnography in the Field of Design. *Human Organization*, 59(4), 377–388.

———. 2002. Collaborative Work: Integrating the Roles of Ethnographers and Designers. In S. Squires and B. Byrne (Eds.), *Creating Breakthrough Ideas: The Collaboration of Anthropologists and Designers in the Product Development Industry*. Westport, CT: Bergin Garvey.

3

OPERATIONALIZING DESIGN ANTHROPOLOGY

How We Know It When We See It

Introduction

What makes design anthropology *a unique form of practice*? To advance a research agenda for design anthropology (Gunn, Otto, & Smith, 2013: xiii) I propose a set of eight principles that can be applied as variables to operationalize the field. Two events that combined elements of design and anthropology (in some cases, in the guise of "ethnography") are presented as vignettes.[1] Building on the work of Kapferer (2010) and others on the exploration of events and situations as a focus of anthropological ethnographic description, the eight principles are applied as a broad set of criteria to assess if and to what extent they are present in each event. This exercise in operationalizing the field provides a means *to know it when we see it*, a critical step in setting parameters and defining the field, even as it continues to evolve.

Disciplinary Evolution: Adapting to Change

For most of the discipline's history, anthropologists have been observers, analysts, and interpreters of cultural and social production and change. Over the last decades of the twentieth century this began to change: the role of anthropologists has shifted from observers, analysts, and interpreters of social structure and culture to participants and agents in the processes of social and cultural transformation. Chapter 1 described how the field has evolved over decades of experimentation, and through intense debate over the role of anthropology in contemporary society, which was restated by Alisse Waterston, president of the American Anthropological Association (2016 press release), in recent communication with the membership "to support the development of anthropological knowledge, to help disseminate that knowledge, and to facilitate the application of knowledge to help solve human problems." Chapter 2 described how the field of design has gone through an equally game-changing evolution. From its twentieth century ties to fine arts and designers' traditional role as "form-givers" and "makers" (Owen, 2006) of objects and images, design has expanded to become a major player in the processes of innovation and future-making. Designers are now intervening in increasingly complex situations that are embedded in multidimensional contexts involving social, cultural, environmental, economic, political, and technological factors. The evolution in design practice includes debates (Dubberly, 2011) about how best to prepare young designers to address wide-ranging situations that involve not only a concern for "the user" of a specific product or service (i.e., human-centered design), but also systems-level concerns about the impact of designed artifacts – broadly defined as products and solutions – on people, the planet, and profit.

Disruptive Change Demands Pluridisciplinary Collaborations

Technology continues to be a major force that has contributed to the evolution of both anthropology and design. New tools and web-based platforms that facilitate collaboration across time and space have radically altered ways in which work is conducted and produced, and has disrupted and reshaped the domains and environments where work is done. The proliferation of sensors, instrumented environments, and the introduction of "Big Data" have engendered new methods in data collection, analysis, and synthesis that call into question the relevance of conventional on-the-ground forms of research. In tandem, globalization in its broadest sense has emerged as a force resulting in assemblages that are connected globally, but play out differently in local contexts (Ong & Collier, 2009).

Technology and globalization have raised our awareness of the complexity of the problems we face and the realization of the limits of approaching problems from a single disciplinary perspective. Instead, multiple disciplinary or *pluridisciplinary*[2] approaches acknowledge different classes of problems, some of which require the integrated perspective of multiple disciplines. Design anthropology is itself a product of this movement.

The designation of pluridisciplinary work advances the recognition by Choi and Pak (2006: 351) that the terms multi-, inter-, and transdisciplinary tend to be used interchangeably and often incorrectly since they indicate distinctly different qualitative states. In their study of how the three terms were applied in academic literature, they consolidated their findings to provide these definitions,

> Multidisciplinarity draws on knowledge from different disciplines but stays within their boundaries. Interdisciplinarity analyzes, synthesizes and harmonizes links between disciplines into a coordinated and coherent whole. Transdisciplinarity integrates the natural, social and health sciences in a humanities context, and transcends their traditional boundaries.
>
> *(Choi & Pak, 2006)*

Strathern (2007) echoes Choi and Pak in acknowledging the crucial distinction among the three terms. Referring to Nowotny's contribution to discussions regarding "the potential of transdisciplinarity" (Gibbons et al., 1994; Nowotny, Scott, & Gibbons, 2001), she writes that

> *Interdisciplinarity*, in the strict sense, points to a framework shared across disciplines to which each contributes a bit. (*Multidisciplinarity*, the simple alignment of skills from different disciplines, is already left behind.) *Transdisciplinarity* implies even more: it brings disciplines together in contexts where new approaches arise out of the interaction between them, but to a heightened degree, in a kind of super compound.
>
> *(2007: 124)*

The qualitative difference between one type of work group and another involves a shift in values and attitudes that allows for a reframing of the problem space, a willingness to accept diverse epistemologies, and openness to considering multiple solutions. Each transition requires a change in the level of investment by team members. *Multidisciplinarity* requires the least investment: each member brings his/ her individual knowledge base; negotiation is primarily in the area of operations, and there is little expectation that members will invest time and energy in changing their perspectives. *Interdisciplinarity* requires a more significant investment of time and energy due to the need for more extensive negotiation in reaching shared understandings, which enables analysis and synthesis to occur across disciplinary boundaries. In the case of *transdisciplinarity*, the requirement for negotiation is very high: all members must be willing to subordinate their individual disciplinary perspectives to achieve a common vision that encompasses the dimensions and dynamics of an entire system. Figure 3.1 illustrates these differences.

Global and historical conditions have influenced the trajectories of design anthropology in the United States, Europe, and other parts of the world. In the United

Multidisciplinary – Additive
Draws on multiple disciplines but stays within disciplinary boundaries

Interdisciplinary – Integrative
Analyzes, synthesizes, harmonizes, links into a coordinated coherent whole

Transdisciplinary - Holistic/Transcendent
Subordinates disciplines, looks at the dynamics of the whole system.

FIGURE 3.1 Types of Pluridisciplinary Teams: Additive, Integrative, and Holistic (Choi & Pak, 2006; visualization created by the author).

States, the confluence of design and anthropology and its introduction to business was brokered by key players, for example, individuals like Rick Robinson, Bill Moddridge, and David Kelley, design firms like IDEO, E-Lab, Doblin, entities such as Xerox PARC, and academic institutions including Stanford's D-school, the Institute of Design (ID) at the Illinois Institute of Technology (IIT), Parsons, and the Savannah College of Art and Design (SCAD). The nascent relationships between designers and anthropologists – most were classically trained Ph.Ds. – were both nurtured and challenged in these early encounters. Although the groundwork for the emergence of design anthropology in the United States was laid during this time, to define design anthropology simply as the direct experience of designers and anthropologists working together severely limits the concept of what the field is today and the potential for its development in the future.

Design Anthropology: "Ethnographies of the Possible"

As an evolving practice that aims for transdisciplinarity, design anthropologists continually experiment with new perspectives on field research, improvise new methods and frameworks, and extract theory as it emerges from data. Building on existing theories of performativity, Halse and Clark (2008) proposed an alternative approach which "advocates a performative ethnography that relocates the inescapable creative aspects of analysis from the anthropologist's solitary working office into a collaborative project space." In their view, this

> ...problematizes the implied authenticity of 'people out there,' and rather favors a performative worldview where people, things and business opportunities are continuously and reciprocally in the making, and where anthropological analysis is only one competence among others relevant for understanding how this making unfolds.
>
> *(2008: 131)*

This position further distinguishes design anthropology from conventional forms of ethnography and design research. In design anthropology practice, ethnography focuses on capturing *the event* as a field of unfolding potential and possibility rather than a description and interpretation of the "here and now" (Halse, 2013: 180). Documenting the context, conditions, and forces around the event is critical in capturing the process of transformation that occurs, but in itself is simply descriptive. This is ethnography in the conventional sense in which the researcher stands outside the event, or possibly plays the role of participant observer: a novice in a kind of apprentice relationship. An expansive ethnographic practice requires an extended role of the researcher as a participant, facilitator, and interventionist in the process of change and transformation (Halse and Boffi, 2016). In the mode of participatory design, this not only requires creating new ways to draw out and articulate "the possible," but also to explore ways to facilitate and guide dynamic transformative action.

Events and Situated Practice

When exploring the potential of a new transdisciplinary field, the challenge presented to practitioners and theorists is to communicate back to a broader audience its unique logic and value. In design anthropology this is often done through project-based case studies that capture an event or series of events that constitute a project. For design anthropologists, the focus on events is related to their significance as a source of emergent potentiality. Halse (2013) and others (Kjaersgaard, 2013) state that this future orientation is central to thinking about the potential of exploratory design practices, such as experimentation, prototyping, and reflective critique, that extend the ethnographic gaze. Shifting from "practices that are given and more or less historically manifest to practices that are suggested, future-oriented, and facilitated through a more or less temporary design event" moves toward a confluence of design and anthropology with the potential for transdisciplinary action. This approach "draws on designerly tools and methods for articulating possibilities in corporeal forms while retaining an ethnographic sensitivity to its social and political implications for the people involved" (Halse, 2013: 183). The integration of designerly and anthropological tools, methods, and theory, which he previously described as "linking an interesting ethnographic observation with an interesting design suggestion" (2008: 3), is at the core of design anthropology, and serves as a benchmark against which the vignettes in this chapter are analyzed.

The vignettes presented in this chapter highlight the connection of situated events to an evolving bigger picture: the dynamic intersection of design, anthropology, engineering, and business, in for-profit, not-for-profit, and public sector enterprise. As a set the vignettes embody facets that shift between depictions of design anthropology and the anthropology of design (Suchman, 2011: 16; Drazin, 2012). They have in common an explicit future orientation and imagine design for change that breaks the patterns of the existing conditions. The vignettes provide opportunities to take an approach in which Kapferer (2010: 1) explains "the aim is toward the exploration of the event as a singularity"

> in which critical dimensions can be conceived as opening to new potentialities in the formation of social realities or what post-structuralists, especially of a Deleuzian persuasion (see Deleuze 2004; Deleuze and Guattari 1987), would describe as the continual becoming of the social as a complex emerging and diversifying multiplicity that is enduringly open and not constrained within some kind of organized, interrelated totality of parts, either as real (existent), imagined, modeled, or projected.
>
> *(Kapferer, 2010: 2)*

Halse and Clark anticipate this sense of reality as "continual becoming"

> ...we believe the world is in a continual process of becoming through our engagements with it, and the user is not authentically 'out there' to

be discovered independently of our interest in the discovery. The user emerges somewhere in the meeting between our search for 'real people,' the practice of the particular participants in our study, and the projected interest in them posed by project stakeholders as possible new areas of use.

(2008: 129)

Before presenting the vignettes, let us review how "the event" has evolved as a significant focus in anthropological inquiry as well as how events figure into design practice.

The Significance of Events and Situations in Anthropological Practice

Kapferer (2010) describes two common and frequently overlapping ways in which events are presented in anthropology and other social sciences. One way presents particular events as examples or illustrations of ethnographies that are either descriptive or that assert a theoretical perspective. In another, events are presented "as happenings or occasions, slices of life, that establish a conundrum or problematic that the presentation of an ethnography and its analysis will solve or otherwise explain" (2010: 1).

Kapferer proposed to extend the use of the case in anthropology beyond the illustration of the event.[3] His "Introduction" to a special issue of *Social Analysis* focused on the anthropological exploration of events and situations inspired by the Manchester School, Turner, and the social philosophy of Deleuze. Kapferer noted early work in this area by Gluckman, Mitchell, and others associated with the Manchester School[4] that explored the anthropological significance of events with a focus on change, which they believed was "the normal condition of all societies" (2010: 7). They advocated for a focus on events as a means of moving beyond conceptual abstractions of society that proposed fixed models as a basis for developing theories to explain the "innumerable and differentiated complexities of everyday life and that, in some sense, must always be speculative." Gluckman's concept of equilibrium shifted the focus from stasis to process, which allowed for "conceiving of the totality that was continually subject to reformulation as a consequence of situated analyses" (2010: 7).

The shift from stasis to process is analogous to the aim to extend the ethnographic gaze, which is at the heart of design anthropological practice and is the key to capturing the position of the anthropologist as both an observer of the transformative process while simultaneously being an active agent within it. McCabe and Briody (2016) refer to this "liminal movement" as central to business anthropology, referring to what Luhmann (2012) calls "second order observation" that "entails active intervention in a situated manner."

Frameworks

The vignettes in this section are examples of "the event" as the continual unfolding of potentialities, each played out as an evolving social drama. Support for this approach draws on existing theoretical frameworks. In imagining the kinds of possible futures that might be accessed by extending the anthropological gaze to encompass peoples' hypothetical worlds, Halse builds on Kapferer's (2010: 10) assertion that Victor Turner should be credited with understanding the event as the locus of creativity and change. Events bridge the "borderline" between ritual and performance theory. Citing Schechner's concept of actuals, Halse writes,

> Drawing on Victor Turner's work on rituals and social dramas (Turner, 1969) Richard Schechner (Schechner, 1988) used "actual" to define those nonmimetic and particularly transformative moments when something contestable happens here and now with irrevocable consequences for the participants.
>
> *(2003: 183)*

Schechner does not presume that change, creativity and transformation are a single, shared imaginary. Nor does he suggest that actuals are totally nonexistent, but rather that something *becomes actualized in the event* through the concrete articulations of things and processes, one of a designer's core competencies. Transformative moments occur in each of the vignettes presented in this chapter, sometimes as a single "Ah hah!," but much more often as a series of accumulated insights that slowly bring forth a new concrete actual. The "liminal movement" of anthropologists between observing the process of transformation occurring as a series of meandering fits and starts and active intervention is a contribution that contemporary anthropologists bring to design anthropological practice.

An Emerging Set of Principles

Design anthropology is practiced in many different ways. *How do we know it when we see it?* Although "measuring" in an exact sense is not possible, an emerging set of principles can be applied to operationalize design anthropology and to create a framework to evaluate projects and discrete events that embody the emerging principles of the design anthropological approach. These include a commitment to a collaborative process that aims to achieve transdisciplinarity; to a participatory design that aims for the inclusion of a wide range of stakeholders; to an iterative design process; to ongoing methodological experimentation and rigorous critique; and to a holistic approach that takes into account social, political, economic, and other implications for people and the planet and both intended and unintended consequences of proposed designed artifacts. The *explicit* aim to achieve transdisciplinary collaboration challenges team members to articulate and demonstrate their individual contributions, and to think beyond disciplinary boundaries subordinating individual disciplinary biases and focusing instead on the dynamics of the holistic system, on what other disciplinary perspectives can contribute, and on how they can add value. Table 3.1 provides a set of principles that serve as general criteria to operationalize design anthropological practice.

TABLE 3.1 Design Anthropology: An Emerging Set of Principles

Emerging principle	Operationalized as
Transformative; Future orientation	The explicit goal of the event engagement is to change or transform the current state of a phenomenon or system. Rather than "future-making," design anthropologists think in terms of "future-in-the-making."
Holistic	This approach studies phenomena as embedded in whole systems rather than as isolated events.
Collaborative	The aim in working with others is to achieve a shared vision and/or to generate solutions to a common problem.
Transdisciplinarity	A commitment to the unity of knowledge that complements disciplinary approaches and facilitates the emergence of new data and new interactions between disciplines. Instead of striving for mastery of several disciplines, transdisciplinarity seeks to create common ground among disciplines as to what they share and the openness as to what lies beyond them (Nicolescu, 1994).
Performative	A worldview that perceives people, things, and opportunities as continuously and reciprocally in the making (Halse & Clark, 2008). Functioning as both a metaphor and an analytical tool, performance is "a bodily practice that produces meaning" and highlights interactions between social actors, or between a social actor (or collective action) and the immediate environment.
Emergent potentiality	The approach takes into account the continuous unfolding of possibilities and the implications for change on social, political, financial, economic, and other dimensions for a broad range of stakeholders and for the planet.
Iterative	The approach implements an iterative design process that includes stages of preparation and planning, exploration, identification of opportunities, ideation, prototyping, testing, and validation. Iteration in this sense implies a willingness to rethink and revise, and to test assumptions throughout the process.
Critical	The core team engages in a process of rigorous critique at each stage of the project to identify and evaluate intended and unintended consequences.

The criteria identified here serves as a set of design principles. Rather than an attempt to codify design anthropology, this instead proposes a way to operation-alize it, enabling us to *know it when we see it*, and distinguish design anthropology from approaches to future-making that promote (or impose) ideas of *what could be*. Rather than a quest for the "Holy Grail" of radical innovation, the design anthropological approach starts at ground level by first gaining an understanding of existing conditions – history, social relations, and material and symbolic cul-tural elements – seeking to understand how people navigate and transform the conditions of their everyday lives. Only after a semblance of grounded "truth" is established can we collectively decipher meaning through a process that identifies patterns and themes in *what is* to imagine *what if* and *what might be.*

This bottom-up approach is grounded in the premise that innovation is essentially a social process that is ubiquitous, dynamic, improvisational, and situational. Innovation is also multidimensional, meaning that it incorporates technologies, economies, social, cultural, political, and environmental factors. Working from the bottom-up, Gunn, Otto, and Smith note that,

> Practitioners of design anthropology follow dynamic situations and social relations and are connected with how people perceive, create, and transform their environments through their everyday activities. This view challenges the idea that design and innovation only refer to the generation of new things as being central to processes of social and cultural change.
>
> *(2013: xiii)*

Adopting this perspective expands the ethnographic gaze to include Halse's "ethnographies of the possible" (2013), and suggests that anthropological practice can find inspiration not only through participating in design practices, "but also in the object of its inquiry, namely that which does not concretely exist, the imaginative" (2013: 181). The challenge of design anthropology is to reimagine and extend theory and ethnographic practice to include what has been described as *ethnographic inquiries into possible futures.*

Towards Future-Making: Vignettes of Cultural Production and Change

The vignettes depicted in this section differ in critical ways. The first is a conference, the second is a workshop hosted by a design school. In only one vignette, the *Design Anthropological Futures* conference, were anthropologists or design anthropologists present in significant numbers. The other two vignettes were led by designers. The events all occurred within the same year. Applying the principles identified in Table 3.1 as variables, each is analyzed by assessing to what degree they are embodied in individual events. A spider web diagram is used to visualize the results. Rather than a definitive analysis of each event, the vignettes are "diagnostic" (Sherry, 1995: 7) in the sense that they illustrate a set of principles that are intended to provoke conversations that further define design anthropology as a distinct form of transdisciplinary practice.

Despite their different purposes, the vignettes share common elements that are used to structure their presentation: each had an explicit purpose, distinctive characteristics, and final outcomes. Each event was explicitly intended to be transformative, either by further defining design anthropology as an emerging transdisciplinary field (Design Anthropological Futures conference), or by generating "synergistic solutions and possibilities" to improve access to health care through a collaborative problem-solving approach (BarnRaise). Both events had a beginning and an end point that was scheduled in advance, allowing them to be captured as discrete events.

Vignette 1: Design Anthropological Futures Conference

The Design Anthropological Futures conference was the last of a series of four events held between April 2014 and August 2015 that was organized by the members of the steering committee of the Research Network for Design Anthropology, an international network of 30-plus individuals, most of whom are associated with academic institutions. The conference was held in Copenhagen at The Royal Danish Academy of Fine Arts School of Design from August 13th to 15th, 2015. The event was promoted by the Research Network for Design Anthropology, the conference organizers, on the KADK website,[5] and posted to various listservs. Registration required a fee of $181 (USD). Participation was open to an international audience and limited to approximately 100 participants from a range of disciplines, most of whom submitted papers that were reviewed for inclusion in one of four themed discussions. The positive response to the conference caused the organizers to close registration so that there could be active rather than passive participation among the attendees.

Referring to the title, the organizers explain that "The concept of futures relates both to the creation of visions and practices of the possible through the transformative processes of anthropology and design, and to the exploration of new frontiers for the field of design anthropology." The conference was selected as one of the vignettes because it provided the opportunity to participate in, and observe first hand, an event focused explicitly on design anthropology, organized by and for people who had an interest in design anthropology, and for those who self-identified as design anthropologists. My role in the conference was as a participant. The paper I submitted (Miller, 2015) envisioned design anthropology as an evolving community of practice (Wenger, 1998), and was included in the session for Theme 1: Ethnographies of the Possible.

Design Anthropological Futures: "Ethnographies of the Possible"

Ethnography in design anthropology is distinctive in that, as Halse argues, ethnography is extended to "ethnographic inquiries of possible futures" (2013: 182) by shifting the temporal frame *from here and now to then and there*. Ethnography in design anthropology is further distinguished by redefining the role of the anthropologist-as-ethnographer. Citing Nafus and Anderson (2006), Halse and Clark (2008) argue that when the competence of anthropologists in industry is predicated primarily on their ability to access the "hinterlands of the real people" that were actually using or might use the product, anthropologists are "relegated to the role of data collector" (2008: 128). Unlike design anthropological practice, in these cases ethnographic fieldwork tends to be handed off to designers, engineers, business strategists, and marketers who use anthropologists' insights to inform product development with little to no participation by the anthropologist.

Analysis and Outcomes

As illustrated in Figure 3.2, the Design Anthropological Futures conference embodies the eight principles identified in Table 3.1. The closing statement on the conference website[6] explicitly addressed *transformation/future orientation, transdisciplinarity, performance,* and *emergent potentiality,* noting that "both the creation of visions and practices of the possible through transformative processes of anthropology and design, and to the exploration of new frontiers for the field of design and anthropology." *Holism, collaboration,* and *criticality* are also addressed in the closing statement,

> The conference explored different perspectives on design anthropology as a holistic and critical approach to complex everyday and societal issues with the aim of creating potential futures with diverse communities and stakeholders.
> *(Design Anthropological Futures Conference website)*

Although not explicit, a willingness to rethink and revise was implied throughout the design of the conference and the conference program. Sessions and

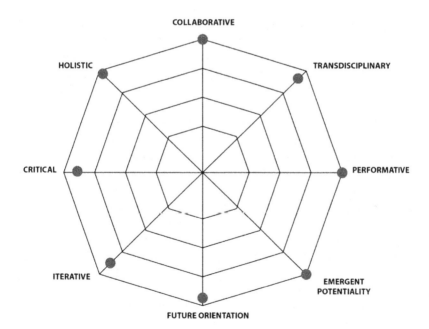

FIGURE 3.2 Design Anthropological Futures: Mapping Emerging Principles of Design Anthropology (spider gram visual by J. Knapp).

breakouts reiterated the rules for engagement, and included opportunities to capture the streams of conversation, linking them to the overall aim of the conference. A book compiled under the auspices of the Research Network for Design Anthropology was intended to be a main outcome of the conference. The benefits for participants included access to content, such as conference papers and session videos, and reconnecting and networking with other researchers that self-identify as design anthropologists.

Vignette 2: BarnRaise

BarnRaise 2015 was a 2-day design event sponsored by the Institute of Design (ID) at the Illinois Institute of Technology (IIT). The event was described as "a uniquely structured maker-conference that connects design firms, community-based organizations, and participants to address a social topic embedded in the Chicago community."[7] My role as both a participant and an observer, arranged in advance with the conference organizers, allowed me to experience BarnRaise as a designer-led event in which neither anthropology nor design anthropology were predominant.

The first BarnRaise was held in the fall of 2014 and was organized and facilitated by ID graduate students. The theme of the 2015 event, Designing for Improved Access to Care, aimed to attract a diverse set of participants: "health care practitioners, designers, health care administrators, graduate students, and beyond." The "beyond" category included individuals and companies, many of which were primarily interested to participate in an event that aspired to "the co-creation of human-centered opportunities for impact" and, secondarily, were interested in the stated theme of access to care. Although the theme specifically targeted projects in Chicago, the event drew a wide range of individual participants, community and design firm "partners," and "strategic partners" from outside the Chicago area.

Described as a "maker-conference," BarnRaise is similar to a "design charrette"[8]: a multiday intensive design collaboration during which teams focus on designing solutions around a particular theme or problem. Facilitated by a design team and sponsored by a mix of private and public sector organizations, participation in design charrettes is typically open to stakeholders that had a direct interest in the project and people who have expertise in a particular aspect of the project (e.g., health care). As a learning and networking event, BarnRaise is open to outside participation, attracting people who want to learn about the design process through firsthand experience: "Under the facilitation of a design firm, participants will work in multidisciplinary teams to develop a user-centered understanding of a problem posed by a community organization and prototype viable solutions" (Figure 3.3).

The emphasis on *making* and *makers* aligns with the trend in active conferencing as an alternative to traditional conference formats in which a presenter delivers (and might read) a paper in front of an audience. The trend towards active conferencing is particularly strong in the design community where the goal is action-based future-making. Creativity is expressed through an iterative process of research, analysis, synthesis, improvisation, and invention with the outcome being some form of designed artifact.

The pace and activity of a "maker conference" contrasts sharply with the traditional academic conference during which scientific research is delivered and discussed from behind a podium to a seated audience of peers. Designer, author, and educator, Charles Owen (2006), used the "maker" concept to describe the difference between design and science by contrasting them as different ways of thinking. Owen described scientific thinkers as *finders* who "exercise their creativity through discovery. Finders are driven to understand, to find explanations for phenomena not well understood." By comparison, designers are *makers* who are "equally creative, but in a different way. They demonstrate their creativity through invention. Makers are driven to synthesize what they know in new constructions, arrangements, patterns, compositions and concepts that bring tangible, fresh expressions of what can be" (2006: 17). Figure 3.4 depicts in broad terms the contrast between design thinking and scientific thinking.

FIGURE 3.3 Addressing Problems Collectively (BarnRaise, 2015).

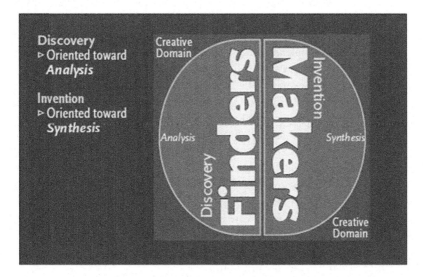

FIGURE 3.4 Two-Domain Creativity Model (Owen, 2007: 17).

Prior to the event, I proposed to the organizers that I would attend as a participant on a design team and also as a researcher. They agreed and encouraged my participation. They were interested in having an opportunity to document BarnRaise 2015. The week before the event I met a designer and Ph.D. candidate at ID who planned to capture the event for her doctoral thesis to discuss our research objectives. She was interested in the event as an opportunity to observe the socialization and training-by-doing of graduate design students as preparation for their professional careers. From my perspective as a participant/researcher, BarnRaise was an opportunity to explore a designer-led workshop event through the lens of design anthropology.

Pre-event: Registration and Team Assignments

BarnRaise was promoted through a variety of channels including an event website, mail lists, face-to-face meetings and social media. Visual language was used to communicate the human-centered and participatory design approach. Sponsors and client organizations were contacted directly by BarnRaise organizers to solicit their participation, sponsorship, and funding.

With the exception of ID students and faculty, all participants paid a registration fee. Once registered, participants were encouraged to complete a short survey that included questions about their background and their particular interests in joining the event. Information collected through the surveys helped the organizers to establish the project teams.

Setting the Stage: Opening Reception

BarnRaise opened with a series of keynote speakers and a reception giving participants the opportunity to meet members of their project teams, and allowed the organizers to frame the event in terms of intent and content. Keynote speakers spoke about the work of designers in tackling the challenges in health care, given the size and complexity of the health care system. Service design was a prominent approach to answering the "big question": *What do people want from their health care system?* Several of the speakers talked about the challenge of communicating the value of design and qualitative research to analysts who worked with quantitative data. Ciara Taylor and Samantha Dempsey from Mad★Pow introduced the topic of ethics in their version of a "Designer's Oath" that would serve as a tool to evoke discussions around ethical questions such as "What's right for me?," "What's right for the patient?," and "What's right for the team?"

On day 1 of the event, participants were able to choose one of two "crash course" presentations before breaking into their teams. I attended the crash course on designing in the health care environment. Alice Ro, a service designer at the Memorial Sloan Kettering Cancer Center in New York, used graphic images (Figures 3.5 and 3.6) to illustrate the profound contrast between norms in design and those in health care environments.

FIGURE 3.5 Contrasting Values: Design and Health Care (photo courtesy of Memorial Sloan Kettering Cancer Center).

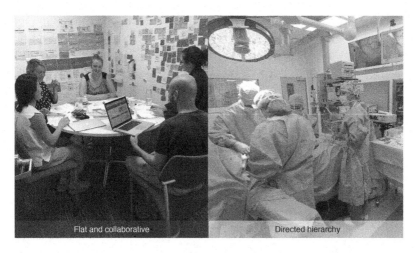

FIGURE 3.6 Contrasting Social Structure: Design and Health Care (photo courtesy of Memorial Sloan Kettering Cancer Center).

The Design Workshop: A "Future-in-the-Making" Event

Describing a design workshop as a sort of rite of passage that facilitates "a transition from *research* to *design*" (Halse & Clark, 2008), Kjaersgaard (2013: 64–65) writes that "inspired by Kapferer (and with him Turner and Deleuze), we might think of this design workshop as a ritualized descent into the virtuality of reality (Kapferer, 2004), a special kind of reality suspended between the *actual* and the *potential*." Kjaersgaard observes that within the "virtual reality" of the workshop existing rules, roles, and hierarchies are temporarily suspended. Nonexpert participants are allowed to reconfigure knowledge "playing with boundaries between the present and the future, the social and the material, at the periphery of their knowledge traditions" (2013: 65). Knowledge, and specifically pieces of knowledge, combined with other knowledge pieces from diverse sources, become the material of design (2013: 57).

This kind of bricolage, characteristic of design workshops in general, was evident during BarnRaise, meeting the principle of *emergent potentiality*. Using the eight principles as a framework to analyze, BarnRaise allows us to position the event in a spider diagram (see Figure 3.8).

Drawing on the traditional barn raising event as a metaphor, the BarnRaise logo[9] (Figure 3.7) suggests a commitment to *collaboration, transformation*, and *future orientation*. The event was promoted, designed, and structured to facilitate *transdisciplinary* interactions among a diverse group of participants.

As a design workshop, BarnRaise embodied the *performative* and *iterative* principles that were evident in the explicit application of design process within each of the working groups. The principle of *holism* was evident to a degree within the project teams. Each project team was led by two facilitators and focused on a particular problem broadly related to access to health care. My project team focused on the Livability Index,[10] AARP's response to the challenge of the aging society in the United States. Working with an AARP staff member, our team studied the Index to understand how the concept of "livability" relates to the challenges *beyond* "the aging society," and considered how the Index might be used by any individual, regardless of age, gender, or physical condition, to assess opportunities and access to education, health care, housing, transportation,

FIGURE 3.7 BarnRaise Logo (2015).

employment opportunities, and community engagement within specific localities. We conducted a focus group with a diverse group of individuals from the local community to explore how the Index was usable for and useful to multiple populations and communities. The client was not able to attend this session. Although the focus group participants were initially quite positive about the Index, once we began the hands-on session, problems with the interface were identified that limited its usability for anyone who was visually or physically impaired. By the end of the session, the group's initial interest and positivity was replaced by a consensus that the Index was not universally usable and that it did not deliver what it promised. *How would this criticism be conveyed to the AARP?* As a common dilemma for design teams that are required to present findings to their clients, this created an opportunity to assess how *critique* and *criticism* would be managed by the project team and the team's facilitators. After our project team debriefed the focus group, the facilitators took responsibility for briefing the client on the results of the session.

The results of applying the eight principles to BarnRaise are depicted in Figure 3.8. The intention is to use the principles as criteria in an exercise in operationalizing design anthropology as a means *to know it when we see it*, and distinguish it from other forms of future-making. This is a critical step in setting parameters and defining the field, even as it continues to evolve.

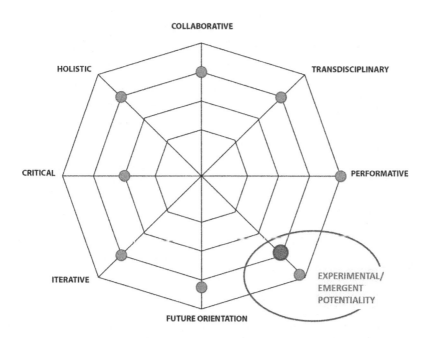

FIGURE 3.8 BarnRaise: Mapping the Emerging Principles of Design Anthropology (spider gram visual by J. Knapp).

Notes

1 Vignettes are defined as short, impressionistic scenes that focus on one moment or give a particular insight into a character, idea, or setting. https://en.wikipedia.org/wiki/Vignette(literature).
2 "The term pluridisciplinary serves not only as a general term, but also as a rubric under which three forms or stages of teaming – multi-, inter- and transdisciplinary – are encompassed" (Miller, 2016).
3 Kapferer later concedes that it is "difficult to avoid" the illustrative dimensions of events. His "suggestion is that an event should not be selected on the basis of its illustrative dimensions or because it is in some way or another a micro example of macro dynamics" (2010: 17).
4 Kapferer refers to "Gluckman's Manchester School" with which J. Clyde Mitchell, Victor Turner, and Kapferer himself, as Gluckman's student, are associated.
5 The Royal Danish Academy of Fine Arts Schools of Architecture, Design and Conservation (accessed June 28, 2016). http://kadk.dk.
6 Closing statement (accessed June 28, 2016). https://kadk.dk/co-design/research-network-design-anthropology/closing-conference-design-anthropological-futures.
7 www.id.iit.edu/barnraise/.
8 https://en.wikipedia.org/wiki/Charrette.
9 BarnRaise logo from Facebook (accessed June 29, 2016). www.facebook.com/barnraise.
10 What is the Livability Index? (Accessed June 29, 2016). https://livabilityindex.aarp.org/livability-defined.

References

Choi, Bernard C.K. and Anita W.P. Pak. 2006. Multidisciplinarity, Interdisciplinarity, and Transdisciplinarity in Health Research, Services, Education and Policy: 1. Definitions, objectives, and evidence of effectiveness. *Clinical & Investigative Medicine*, 2006 (6), 361–364.

Deleuze, Gilles. 2004. *Difference and Repetition*. Trans. Paul R. Patton. New York: Continuum.

Deleuze, Gilles and Felix Guattaro. 1987. *A Thousand Plateaus: Capitalism and Schizophrenia*. Trans. Brian Massumi. Minneapolis: University of Minnesota Press.

Drazin, Adam. 2012. Design Anthropology: Working on, with and for Digital Technologies. In H. Horst and D. Miller (Eds.), *Digital Anthropology*, Chapter 12. Oxford: Berg.

Dubberly, Hugh. 2011. Input for Updating the ICOGRADA Design Education Manifesto. *AICOGRADA Design Education Manifesto*, 76–81.

Gibbons, Michael, Camille Limoges, Helga Nowotny, Simon Schwartzman, Peter Scott, and Martin Trow. 1994. *The New Production of Knowledge: The Dynamics of Science and Research in Contemporary Societies*. London: Sage.

Gunn, Wendy, Ton Otto, and Rachel C. Smith (Eds.). 2013. *Design Anthropology: Theory and Practice*. New York: Bloomsbury.

Halse, Joachim. 2013. Ethnographies of the Possible. In W. Gunn, T. Otto, and R.S. Smith (Eds.), *Design Anthropology: Theory and Practice*, 180–196. New York: Bloomsbury.

Halse, Joachim and Brandon Clark. 2008. Design Rituals and Performative Ethnography. *Ethnographic Praxis in Industry Conference Proceedings*, 2008(1), 128–145.

Halse, Joachim and Laura Boffi. 2016. Design Interventions as a Form of Inquiry. In R.C. Smith, K.T. Vangkilde, M.G. Kjaersgaard, T. Otto, J. Halse, and T. Binder (Eds.), *Design Anthropological Futures*. New York: Bloomsbury.

Kapferer, Bruce. 2004. Ritual Dynamics and Virtual Practice: Beyond Representation and Meaning. *Social Analysis*, 48(2), 35–54.

————. 2010. Introduction: In the Event-Toward an Anthropology of Generic Moments. *Social Analysis*, 54(3), 1–27.

Kjaersgaard, Mette G. 2013. (Trans)forming Knowledge and Design Concepts in the Design Workshop. In W. Gunn, T. Otto, and R.S. Smith (Eds.), *Design Anthropology: Theory and Practice*, 51–67. New York: Bloomsbury.

Luhmann, Niklas. 2012. *Introduction to Systems Theory*. Cambridge: Polity.

McCabe, Maryann and Elizabeth Briody. 2016. Working in Liminal States: Fluidity and Transformation in Organizations. *Journal of Business Anthropology*, Special Issue (2), 1–12.

Miller, Christine. 2015. *What's Anthropological about Design Anthropology? A Personal Reflection*. Paper Presented at the Design Anthropological Futures Conference, Copenhagen, Denmark.

————. 2016. Towards Transdisciplinarity: Liminality and the Transitions Inherent in Pluridisciplinary Collaborative Work. *Journal of Business Anthropology*, Special Issue (2), 1–23.

Nafus, Dawn and ken Anderson. 2006. The Real Problem: Rhetorics of Knowing in Corporate Ethnographic Research. *Ethnographic Praxis in Industry Conference Proceedings* (1), 244–258. Malden, MA: Blackwell Publishing.

Nicolescu, Basarab. 1994. Charter of Transdisciplinarity. In B. Nicolescu, E. Morin, and L. de Freitas (Eds.), Presented at the First World Congress on Transdisciplinarity, Convento de Arrabida, Portugal.

Nowotny, Helga, Peter Scott, and Michael Gibbons. 2001. *Re-thinking Science: Knowledge and the Public in an Age of Uncertainty*. Cambridge: Polity.

Ong, Aihwa and Stephen Collier (Eds.). 2009. *Global Assemblages: Technology, Politics, and Ethics as Anthropological Problems*. Malden, MA: Blackwell Publishing.

Owen, Charles. 2007. Design Thinking: Notes on Its Nature and Use. *Design Research Quarterly*, 2(1), 16–27.

Schechner, Richard. 1988. *Performance Theory*. New York: Routledge.

Sherry, John F., Jr. 1995. *Contemporary Marketing and Consumer Behavior: An Anthropological Sourcebook*. Thousand Oaks, CA: Sage.

Strathern, Marilyn. 2007. Interdisciplinarity: Some Models from the Human Sciences. *Interdisciplinary Science Review*, 32(2), 123–134.

Suchman, Lucy. 2011. Anthropological Relocations and the Limits of Design. *Annual Review of Anthropology*, 40, 1–18.

Turner, Victor. 1969. *Ritual Process: Structure and Anti-Structure*. Hawthorne, NY: Aldine de Gruyter.

Waterston, Alisse. 2016. AAA Implements Action on Israel-Palestine. Press Release on June 24, 2016.

Wenger, Etienne. 1998. *Communities of Practice: Learning, Meaning, and Identity*. Cambridge: Cambridge University Press.

4

MAPPING DESIGN ANTHROPOLOGY

Introduction

This chapter is about the diffusion of an innovation known as design anthropology and its prospects as an emerging transdisciplinary field. Having proposed a method for operationalizing design anthropology in the previous chapter, here I address the final aim of the book, to contribute to a vision of design anthropology as an emerging transdisciplinary field and global community of practice comprised of regionalized collaborative innovation networks. The chapter was written in collaboration with Ken Riopelle who provided analytical expertise in social network analysis (SNA). We applied dynamic network analysis (DNA), a scientific field that brings together traditional SNA and network science to investigate the human and nonhuman actors (i.e., people and institutions) that have contributed to design anthropological practice and theorizing.

We begin by establishing a basis for design anthropology as a unique branch of knowledge production. Why is this necessary and what does it contribute to our understanding of the field? Should not this be at the beginning of the book? Instead, it comes at the end – why? The previous chapters have described how two established disciplines evolved and converged, and, as a result, a new transdisciplinary field has emerged. How might we know if this new field is diffusing, developing, and maturing? Is design anthropological theory and practice being shared and discussed? Who are the practitioners? Who (and what) is influencing the direction the field is taking? We get a sense of the growth and diffusion of design anthropology and the people and institutions that are promoting its development by applying the methods described in the following sections.

Design Anthropology: Discipline, Subject Area, or Research Strategy?

Although design anthropology has been described as "an emerging transdisciplinary field" (Otto & Smith, 2013:10), does it qualify as a discipline? Is it a research strategy or a subfield? Although the term *discipline* tends to be applied loosely, there are established criteria that are used to determine if and when a field of study and knowledge production is recognized as a discipline. A broad set of generally accepted indicators can also be applied to determine if and to what extent a new branch of knowledge is an academic or scientific discipline. These indicators include dedicated conferences and seminars, funding and sponsorship, journals, research agendas, recognized experts, professional societies and organizations, academic courses and programs focused on the subject area, and dissertations that specifically focus on the subject area. A relatively quick determination based on the indicators listed above can be completed manually.

A more rigorous formal classification method that is used to determine if and when a field of study qualifies as a discipline is based on an extensive search of "citable items." For example, Thomson Reuters' Web of Science (WoS) is a widely recognized resource that provides this type of formal analysis.[1] The WoS tracks

TABLE 4.1 GIPP Mapping Table (excerpt): The Web of Science Schema is Comprised of 252 SCs in Science, Social Sciences, Arts, and Humanities

		GIPP Discipline			
Arts & Humanities	*Clinical, Pre- Clinical & Health*	*Engineering & Technology*	*Life Sciences*	*Physical Sciences*	*Social Sciences*
Art	Allergy	Acoustics	Agricultural Economics & Policy	Astronomy/ Astrophysics	Anthropology
Architecture	Anesthesiology	Automation & Control Systems	Agricultural Engineering	Chemistry, Analytical	Archaeology
Classics	Audiology & Speech-Language Pathology	Computer Science, Artificial Intelligence	Agriculture, Dairy & Animal Science	Chemistry, Applied	Area Studies
Cultural Studies	Cardiac & Cardiovascular Syatems	Computer Science, Cybernetics	Agriculture, Multidisciplinary	Chemistry, Inorganic & Nuclear	Asian Studies
Dance	Clinical Neurology	Computer Science, Hardware & Architecture	Agronomy	Chemistry, Medicinal	Business

the emergence of new subject categories (SCs) based on "citable items" that include journal articles, conference proceedings, and reviews (Leydesdorff, Carley, & Rafols, 2013). The Science and Social Science Index (SCI + SoSCI), which is updated periodically, currently includes 252 SCs across six broad areas (Table 4.1). Classifying and cataloging emerging subject areas is a complex ontological task. Not only is the terminology confusing (2013: 589–590), but the process is also dynamic. The rate of new subject areas is steadily increasing as science becomes more interdisciplinary (Porter & Rafols, 2009). Some SCs, for example, Chemistry, have split off into separate categories while others may be eliminated.

In the section of the GIPP Mapping Table shown in Table 4.1, Anthropology is listed as a WoS SC under the discipline Social Sciences. Archaeology is also recognized as SC. However, none of Anthropology's other branches or subfields – Biological Anthropology, Cultural Anthropology, and Linguistic Anthropology – are listed as SCs. Design does not appear under any of the six disciplines as SC.

Basic Web Search: Google Ngram

We first used several readily available web-based analytic tools to collect data from the Internet to provide a broad-brush preliminary view of design anthropology. Entering the phrase "design anthropology" in the Google Books Ngram Viewer will display a graph showing how that phrase has occurred in a corpus of books over a selected time range between 1880 and 2008.[2] Multiple phrases can be entered for comparison between topics. Two-word phrases are called bigrams; single-word phrases are unigrams. Searches can be run in a range of languages. The Ngram searches displayed in Figures 4.1–4.3 are in English and are not case

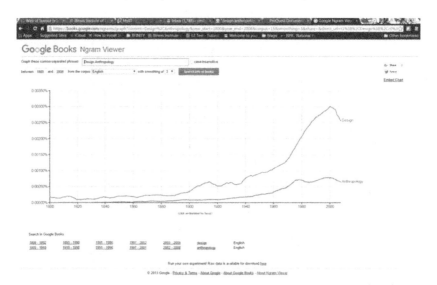

FIGURE 4.1 Ngram Search Results for "Design" and "Anthropology" Between 1800 and 2008.

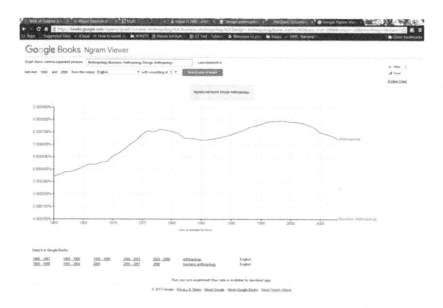

FIGURE 4.2 Ngram Graph Comparing "Anthropology," "Business Anthropology," and "Design Anthropology" Between 1960 and 2008.

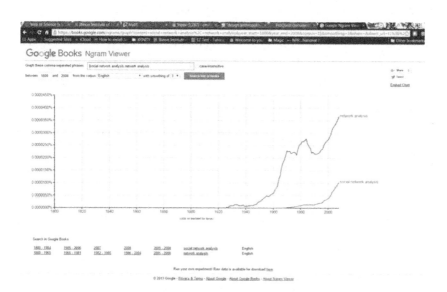

FIGURE 4.3 Ngram Results Comparing "Network Analysis" and "Social Network Analysis" Between 1800 and 2008.

sensitive. We also searched for the phrase "social network analysis," a relatively new interdisciplinary field, to serve as a comparable subject area.

Although several books have been written on design anthropology, none were published before 2009, so the search for "design anthropology" did not yield an Ngram. Entering "design" and "anthropology" separately generated the graph in Figure 4.1 showing that the phrase "design" occurs more frequently than "anthropology," especially since 1960. The difference was dramatic when we shortened shifting the search parameters from 1990 to 2008.

"Design anthropology" is sometimes described as a subset of "business anthropology." An Ngram of three phrases – "anthropology," "business anthropology," and "design anthropology" (Figure 4.2) – shows that business anthropology does have a minimal presence compared to anthropology, but design anthropology does not appear at all.

By comparison, we entered the phrases "social network analysis" and "network analysis" which produced the Ngram in Figure 4.3. Not surprisingly, the phrase "network analysis" has a greater presence than "social network analysis," which is considered a subfield.

Google Scholar and ProQuest

A series of searches in Google Scholar were conducted using multiple terms including "design anthropology," "design + anthropology," and "design and anthropology." As in the Ngram searches, we used "social network analysis," a relatively new interdisciplinary field, as a search term to serve as a comparable subject area. Although Google Scholar searches will produce different results based on factors such as the date on which they are run,[3] they can provide an estimate of the occurrence of the term in articles and other publications. The results of Google Scholar searches are listed in Table 4.2.

TABLE 4.2 Google Scholar Term Search (July 8, 2016)

	Sort criteria	*Number of hits*
"Design Anthropology"	Sort by relevance-anytime	1,070
	Sort by date	38
	Sort by custom date 1990–2016	1,060
	Sort by custom date 1980–2016	1,070
"Social Network Analysis"	Sort by relevance-anytime	168,000
	Sort by date	1,990
	Sort by custom date 1990–2016	79,200
	Sort by custom date 1980–2016	85,400

Note: Terms in quotes are specific search terms.

A Google Scholar search of "design anthropology" and "dissertation" revealed four dissertations on design anthropology from Denmark (Pedersen, 2007; Clark, 2008; Halse, 2008; Kjaersgaard, 2011) and one from the UK (O'Toole, 2015). A similar search on ProQuest[4] resulted in one dissertation which is mentioned above (O'Toole, 2015) and a M.S. thesis from the University of North Texas (Shade, 2015).[5]

The high-level searches described above suggest that as a unique field of knowledge production, "design anthropology" has not achieved the level of SC or discipline. However, finer-grained searches reveal that "design anthropology" does meet some of the indicators of an emerging field, for example, having dedicated conferences, seminars, publications, and dissertations. An investigation that draws on large data sets sourced from the Internet allows us to apply more rigorous analytic tools to visualize networks of people and institutions, giving us a snapshot of the breadth and depth of design anthropology and its relative maturity as an emerging field.[6] In the following section, data collected in the preliminary *telescopic* searches described above are used for deeper *microscopic* analysis by applying network analysis tools.

Social Network Analysis of Design Anthropology Events and Contributors

A set of 12 "events" was selected to represent significant design anthropology activities between 2011 and 2016. Each of the 12 events was explicitly identified as "design anthropology" either in the title or, in the case of the series of three seminars, a sub-event of a larger event. The conference "Ethnography + Design: Mutual Provocations" (#9) is an exception in that it does not explicitly refer to design anthropology in the title, but mentions design anthropology in the content. The decision to include it was based on the fact that several of the individuals listed as Invited Speakers are key contributors in other events.

Data Description

Table 4.3 lists the 12 significant design anthropology events identified for this analysis. The Events include conferences (#7 and 9), seminars (#3, 4, and 5), an invited panel (#10), edited books (#6, 8, 11, and 12), and fixed committees and networks (#1 and 2). Although there have been other venues that are significant in spreading information about design anthropology,[7] for example, the "AnthroDesign"[8] mailing list started by Natalie Hanson in 2002, the 12 events we selected for analysis are explicit in associating with the phrase "design anthropology." Also, the events[9] were posted on the Internet with the lists of contributors and attendees' names available from a public source, such as a website or a list of author names and their affiliations at the time of the event or publication.

The data has been posted as a companion to this chapter (https://designanthropology.live/). We invite those who are interested to download the network and site data and do additional analysis on their own.

TABLE 4.3 Design Anthropology Significant Events from 2011 to 2016

List #number	Lists name and sorted by year	Count	Type event	Year
11	Design Anthropology: Object Culture for the 21st Century (2011)	19	Edited Book	2011
12	Design and Anthropology (2012)	21	Edited Book	2012
1	Research Network for Design Anthropology: Steering Committee	7	Committee	2013
2	Research Network for Design Anthropology: Participants	30	Network	2013
6	Design Anthropology: Theory and Practice (2013): Editors Contributors	18	Edited Book	2013
3	Seminar 1: Ethnographies of the Possible (April 2014): Presenters	16	Seminar	2014
4	Seminar 2: Interventionist Speculation (August 2014): Presenters	25	Seminar	2014
5	Seminar 3: Collaborative Formation of Issues (January 2015): Presenters	19	Seminar	2015
7	Design Anthropological Futures Conference Copenhagen, DK August 13–14, 2015: Position Papers and Posters	87	Conference	2015
8	Design Anthropological Futures (available November 2016): Editors, Contributors, and Reviewers	32	Edited Book	2016
9	Ethnography + Design Mutual Provocations Conference. San Diego, October 27–29, 2016: Invited Speakers	13	Conference	2016
10	AAA Annual Meeting Minneapolis, November 16–20, 2016: Design Anthropology Panel	8	Invited Panel	2016
	Total	295		

Social Network Analysis

The 12 events and the people who contributed to them were converted into a node and link list[10] for SNA. Each event was given an ID number. The 295 contributors were consolidated into an unduplicated list of 180 individuals and likewise assigned a unique ID number. Contributors include people who participated in a conference, seminar, or speaker panel, as well as those who provided a chapter or edited a book. Contributions were not weighted. A link list was constructed by indicating who participated in each event. A total of 295 links were created.

The SNA software, MultiNet/Negopy, was used to analyze the data. Figure 4.4 is a projection of 180 unique people involved in the 12 events. The normal eigenvector[11] display was used to sort the people and events in order of their degree of

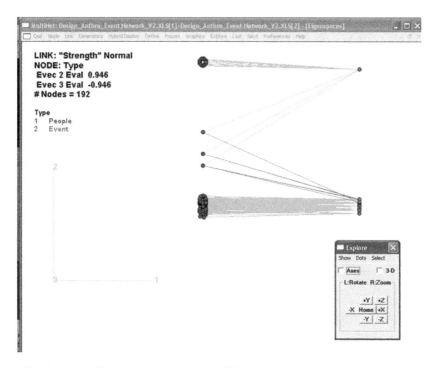

FIGURE 4.4 MultiNet Projection of the 180 People Contributing to 12 Design Anthropology Events from 2011 to 2016.

connection. The people and events at the top and bottom of Figure 4.4 are more peripheral, while those in the center are most central. The dots on the left represent the people and the dots on the right represent the events.

The first observation is that there is one event at the top separated from the rest, and it has a unique set of people attached to it, but it is connected to other events by three people who serve as liaisons or bridges.

Figure 4.5 is the same projection, but with the names displayed. The upper lone event (#11) is the Edited Book 2011: *Design Anthropology: Object Culture for the 21st Century* (Clarke, 2011). Three people, Jo-Anne Bichard, Jamer Hunt, and Alison Clarke, connect this event to the other event cluster below. Specifically, Jo-Anne Bichard attended event # 7 and 11, Jamer Hunt attended event #2, 4, and 11, and Alison Clarke attended event #2, 5, 8, and 11 from the list in Table 4.3.

Table 4.4 lists the 19 people who contributed to event #11, the Edited Book 2011: *Design Anthropology: Object Culture for the 21st Century* (Clarke, 2011).

Next, we used Negopy, a software tool within MultiNet that has a group-detecting or clustering algorithm, to further investigate the data. Negopy refined the larger cluster below into two more groups. Figure 4.6 represents another projection with three distinct groups labeled A, B, and C. Group A is the Edited Book 2011 set of the 19 contributors of which three, Jo-Anne Bichard, Jamer Hunt, and Alison Clarke, serve as liaisons to Group C. Group B

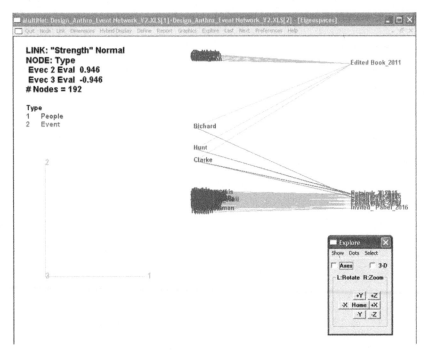

FIGURE 4.5 MultiNet Projection of the 180 People Contributing to 12 Design Anthropology Events from 2011 to 2016, with Names.

represents 112 people who participated in only one of the 11 remaining events. Group C represents the Core Group of the 11 remaining events and 52 people who have participated in two or more events, including the three liaisons.

In addition, in Group C, the people who occupy the most central positions are: Ton Otto, Rachel C. Smith, George Marcus, Brandon Clark, Sissel Olander, Zoy Annastassakis, Mike Anusas, Melissa Caldwell, Elisa Giaccardi, Carl DiSalvo, Tau Ulv Lenskjold, Ramia Mazé, and Mette Gislev Kjærsgaard.

Google Sites Search

We then analyzed the institutional actors – the institutions that were listed with key contributors – to examine the extent to which they were promoting and supporting design anthropology on the Web. To find out we collected the 27 URLs associated with each person that was listed as either a member of the Steering Committee (event #1) or as a network participant (event #2) for the Research Network for Design Anthropology. We chose to use the URLs for the people associated with the Research Network for Design Anthropology first, because many of the people on these lists were identified as Core Contributors and second, because the information is publicly available.[12] We also included three URLs that are not associated with single individuals: the URL for the Research Network for

TABLE 4.4 Edited Book 2011 Contributors (event #11)

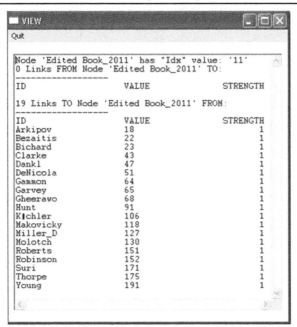

```
■ VIEW                                    [_][□][X]
Quit

Node 'Edited Book_2011' has "Idx" value: '11'
0 Links FROM Node 'Edited Book_2011' TO:
----------------
ID                    VALUE              STRENGTH

19 Links TO Node 'Edited Book_2011' FROM:
----------------
ID                    VALUE              STRENGTH
Arkipov               18                 1
Bezaitis              22                 1
Bichard               23                 1
Clarke                43                 1
Dankl                 47                 1
DeNicola              51                 1
Gammon                64                 1
Garvey                65                 1
Gheeravo              68                 1
Hunt                  91                 1
Kichler               106                1
Makovicky             118                1
Miller_D              127                1
Molotch               130                1
Roberts               151                1
Robinson              152                1
Suri                  171                1
Thorpe                175                1
Young                 191                1
```

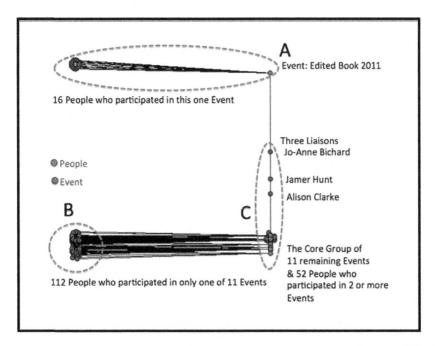

FIGURE 4.6 Negopy Clustering of 180 People Contributing to 12 Design Anthropology Events from 2011 to 2016.

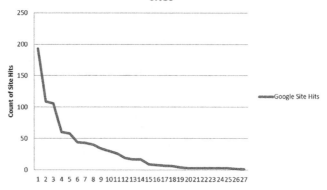

FIGURE 4.7 Google Sites Hits for 27 URLs.

Design Anthropology that is hosted on the KADK website and the URLs of two established conferences that are not explicitly focused on design anthropology, but have provided venues where design anthropologists have presented their work.

We searched the Web using Google Sites to find the number of hits for each URL for the phrase "Website URL AND 'design anthropology.'" All searches were conducted between July 21 and 23, 2016. The results are displayed in Figure 4.7.

The results show a cumulative count of 851 hits for the 27 URLs with 55 percent of the hits coming from four institutions.[13] The highest number of hits was on the Aarhus University website (193), followed by UC Berkeley's ARC lab (109), Swinburne University of Technology (106), and The Royal Danish Academy of Fine Arts (60). We also considered that "design anthropology" would be less likely to be found on the non-English websites. Overall, it is clear there is a great deal of variability across these sites – 14 URLs had less than 10 hits suggesting that the topic design anthropology is not a concentration at that institution. There could be a variety of reasons for this, such as the issue of language that was mentioned previously. However, the most likely reason is that there are only a few people, or perhaps only one person, contributing to design anthropology at that institution. The results for the three URLs that are not associated with a particular individual showed that the EPIC People website had a high number of hits (58), indicating strong support for topic design anthropology.

Discussion of Findings

The aim of our analysis was to answer key questions regarding the status of design anthropology as a unique field of knowledge production, about its communication through various channels, and its diffusion among a variety of networks.

The first question regarding design anthropology's status was answered with a series of preliminary Web searches. As an emerging field, design anthropology does not meet the formal criteria established by the WoS to qualify as a discipline or subject area. As a new field with no dedicated journals, it does not meet the threshold of "citable items" when compared to well-established subject areas, for example, Area Studies given in Table 4.1. However, we found that design anthropology met most of the informal generally accepted indicators of an emerging field (Table 4.5).

TABLE 4.5 Indicators of an Emerging Field

Indicator	Present/not present	Event or source
Conferences	✓	Design Anthropology Futures Conference (2015)
Seminars	✓	Seminar 1: Collaborative Formation of Issues (2014)
		Seminar 2: Interventionist Speculation (2014)
		Seminar 3: Ethnographies of the Possible (2015)
Invited panels	✓	Design Anthropology: Discovery and Evidence of Emerging Pathways in Anthropology (2016)
Funding	✓	Two-year funding from the Danish Research Council (2013–2015)a
Journals		
Research agendas	✓	In process, especially through the seminars and conference organized by the Research Network for Design Anthropology
Recognized experts	✓	The list of Invited Speakers (event #11) indicates that there is an emerging group of individuals recognized for their expertise
Membership-based organizations and societies		
Focused academic courses/programs	✓	University of Aberdeen (MSc Design Anthropology; Ph.D. program)
		University of Southern Denmark (Ph.D. program)
		Swinburne University (Design Anthropology MA Program) until 2016
		University of North Texas (ANTH 4701_008: Design Anthropology)
		University College London (MA Materials. Anthropology. Design program)
Focused dissertations and theses	✓	Pedersen (2007); Clark (2008); Halse (2008); Kjaersgaard (2011); Shade (2015)

aFunding from the Danish Research Council provided support for a conference and seminar series with the aim to "to identify the potentials and challenges" and to map a research agenda. "About the Research Network for Design Anthropology." (Accessed July 25, 2016.) https://kadk.dk/en/research-network-design-anthropology.

Design Anthropology's COINs and CoPs

We refer to three conceptual/theoretical frameworks related to collaboration, collective intelligence, innovation networks, and the diffusion of innovation to translate the findings. Using SNA tools, we were able to identify the 13 Core Contributors who were most central in the network of 180 People. The 13 Core Contributors were either members of the Steering Committee of the Research Network for Design Anthropology or listed as network participants. Over the period between 2011 and 2016 they were the most active contributors to significant Design Anthropology Events, forming a nucleus or what could be described as a *Collaborative Innovation Network* or COIN (Gloor, 2006). A COIN is a group of self-organizing, self-motivated people who share a collective vision. Enabled by the Web, members of a COIN can collaborate to achieve a common goal by the sharing of ideas, information, and work. (2006: 4) However, a COIN can be colocated or virtual. COINs are not a new phenomenon; they have existed throughout history.

Members of a COIN develop new ideas, collectively making the knowledge they create and share collaboratively greater than what could be produced if members were working alone. High levels of participation and trust are needed for a COIN to function successfully. Collaboration occurs "under a strict code of ethics" that includes internal transparency and direct communication between members as opposed to a hierarchical or bureaucratic chain of command (2006: 11). COINs are self-organizing as opposed to being driven by a command-and-control style organization. Members are motivated by intrinsic rewards rather than the promise of monetary or similar forms of compensation. Citing examples such as the development of Linux and the World Wide Web, Gloor argues that under these conditions, COINs constitute "the most successful engines of innovation ever" (2006: 4).

The 13-member Core Group embodies the three primary activities of a COIN. They *innovate* through collective creativity, they *collaborate*, and they *communicate* among themselves outside a formal hierarchy (2006: 12). The seminar series and conference organized by the Research Network for Design Anthropology provide a good example of innovating through collaborative creativity, an intention that was made clear in the open invitation to researchers, and the exploratory nature of the events described in the website content. During the conference event (#7), the facilitators strongly encouraged discussion and engagement among participants and with the artifacts (i.e., papers, posters, and interactive exhibits). As a participant and contributor, this engendered the sense of participating in creating something bigger from the sum of the individual contributions.

The three key roles within a COIN – *creators, communicators* and *collaborators* – can be applied to describe the network of contributors to the 12 Design Anthropology Events. *Creators* are individuals who not only come up with the visionary ideas, but are also able to attract the attention of others. The 13 members of the Core Group and others on the Steering Group that conceived of the Research Network for Design Anthropology, and secured funding from the Danish Research Council fit the role of *creators*. The creation of the Research Network served as a means of consolidating individual energy to create a vortex of energy to attract the attention of interested individuals. Using the swarming behavior of bees as an analogy, Gloor (2006: 20–21) describes how *creators* get others excited, raising the level of the energy necessary for individuals to invest time and energy in exploring a new field. Some of these individuals become *communicators* who spread the buzz and serve as ambassadors carrying the invention – the new idea – over the tipping point (Gladwell, 2000), the moment of critical mass. *Communicators* form a diverse group whose personal ties bridge other networks. People with relatively large networks make excellent *communicators*. *Collaborators* form the glue of the COIN working to see that the vision becomes a reality. We found that in each of the 12 events, a group of *collaborators* was present to do the often invisible work of organizing seminars, conferences, panels, and edited books. Without their commitment there would be no means for people to come together to create and share knowledge that would further the development of design anthropology.

A COIN is actually an ecosystem of three interrelated communities that are illustrated in Figure 4.8: the Core Group or collaborative innovation network (COIN), the Collaborative Learning Network (CLN), and the Collaborative Interest Network (CIN). Our analysis suggests that the clusters that formed Groups A, B, and C align with the COIN model. The COIN is made up of a small Core Group of dedicated individuals. This would include the 13 Core Contributors who are members of Group C and occupy the most central position in the network by contributing to the most events. In this analysis we used the cumulative number of contributions to the 12 events as an indicator of personal commitment. The CLN is a larger group that shares a common interest, and members that want "to get to know and learn from like-minded people." This would be the remaining 39 people in Group C who contributed to two or more events. The CIN can be a very large group. In this network, the CIN is composed of the 112 people who share an interest, but did not contribute to more than one event. Together the COIN, CLN, and CIN form what Gloor calls a Collaborative Knowledge Network (CKN), "a high speed feedback loop in which the innovative results of

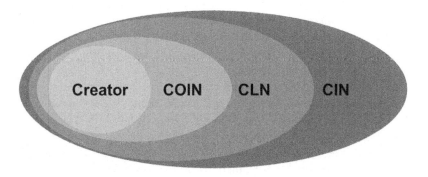

FIGURE 4.8   Adaptation of Gloor's COIN Model used with Permission of the Designer (Jara, 2011).

the COINs are immediately taken up and tested, refined or rejected by the learning and interest networks, and fed back to the originating COINs." Together the communities support the growth of a CKN ecosystem, "the main mechanism by which COIN innovations are carried over the tipping point" (2006: 127–128).

The open environment of the seminars (events #3, 4, and 5) and conference (event #7), organized and facilitated by members of the Research Network for Design Anthropology, provide an example of a CKN feedback loop. Unlike the traditional presentation model of "one-to-many," paper contributions were organized by themes, and presented in sessions called "Discussions" that encouraged active engagement and exchange. The open "many-to-many" format created a feedback loop in which ideas were shared and responded to on the spot, with one contribution leading seamlessly into the next. Rather than the typical poster session, "Interactive Exhibitions" followed a similar mode of active engagement where contributors held short workshops that allowed conference participants to interact with the exhibit content with the explicit aim of "furthering the discussion about design anthropological practices."[14] Conversations continued after the conference, in most cases at a distance, sometimes generating invitations and opportunities to continue the discussions to further design anthropological theory and practice in other events (# 8, 9, and 10).

The COIN, CLN, and CIN networks are fluid and mostly informal and permeable. Membership is dynamic and, consequently, changes over time due to factors previously noted that might affect a person's position, such as physical distance, travel budgets, time, knowing about, or being invited to contribute to an event.

Through the mutual engagement among Contributors, collective negotiation, and the development of a growing repertoire of resources, design anthropology embodies the characteristics of an expanding Community of Practice (CoP) (Lave & Wenger, 1991; Wenger, 1999). As individuals commit time and energy by contributing to edited books or presenting at conferences, seminars, or panels, their position within the community changes. Figure 4.9 illustrates what Lave and Wenger described as the trajectories of participation and nonparticipation. The differences between "peripherality" and "marginality" are understood as trajectories that illustrate the significance of participation or nonparticipation. Peripherality can move in a trajectory that brings members closer to the core of the group through their increased participation by contributing to more events. Peripherality can also describe a trajectory that orbits a member at the edge of the group due to their minimal participation. Both of these trajectories are fluid and can change as a result of an individual's personal reasons or due to changes within the community of practice. Marginality is a state of nonparticipation which prevents full participation (Wenger, 1999: 166). The trajectory for marginality is directed to the edge of the community rather than the center. For example, a person whose skills and competencies are significantly lower than others in the group might be marginalized. This could include individuals whose language skills prevent their participation in the community of practice.

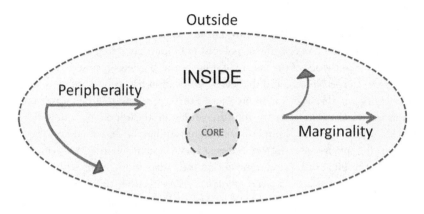

FIGURE 4.9 Relations of Participation and Non-Participation.
Source: Adapted from Wenger (1998: 167).

Contextual issues can also impact peripherality and marginality; for example, we know that the physical location of events and shrinking institutional travel budgets can constrain people's opportunities to participate and contribute to conferences, seminars, and panels that are located far from home. Also, work commitments, family issues, or personal illness are likely to take priority over community engagement.

The concept of CoPs provides a useful framework for discussing the analysis of design anthropology social networks. The emphasis on social participation, dimensions of learning, and trajectories of peripherality and marginality align conceptually with the basic tenets of COINs. In the next section we will introduce diffusion theory to explain how design anthropology theory and practice are being communicated and spread to other communities and networks.

Tracking the Diffusion of Innovation

> Think of something new, you've got an invention. Change the world in which we live, you've got an innovation.
>
> *Arno Penvias, Venture Partner, New Enterprise Associates*
> *Nobel Laureate in Physics 1978*
> *Quoted Sept – Oct 1999, MIT*

So far, we have described two conceptual/theoretical frameworks related to collaboration, collective intelligence, and innovation networks. Diffusion Theory (Rogers, 2003) provides a third framework which helps to explain the dissemination of design anthropological theory and practice through an increasing number of networks. The four main elements of Diffusion Theory – the invention or idea, communication channels, social systems, and adoption over time – can be applied to our analysis to show how information and knowledge is being communicated and shared through multiple networks and channels.

Before Diffusion Theory, anthropologist H.G. Barnett (1953) attempted to formulate a general theory of the nature of innovation. Barnett proposed that innovation is a *mental phenomenon*, and that every innovation has its beginning as an *idea*, regardless of whether it is a new product or service, a new religion, a movement such as environmentalism or, in the case of design anthropology, a new field of knowledge production. Through a series of case studies, he described how the new idea (i.e., the invention) is introduced to a social system where it goes through a process that results in adoption, reinvention (i.e., adaptation), or rejection. Barnett framed innovation as a *social process of cultural change*. Rather than a mechanical or technical challenge, he argued that "The real challenge for a general theory of innovation lies in the realm of behavior, belief, and concept" (1953: 12).

Rogers also focused on social aspects and cultural change as essential components of the innovation process. He defined diffusion as "the process in which an innovation is communicated through certain channels over time among the members of a social system" (2003: 5). Communication is defined as "a process in which participants create and share information with one another in order to reach a mutual understanding." A communication channel "is the means which messages get from one individual to another" (2003: 36). Rogers notes that communication in this sense "implies a process of convergence or divergence as two or more individuals exchange information in order to move toward each other (or apart) in the meanings that they give to certain events." Diffusion, he argues, "is a special type of communication in which the messages are about a new idea. This newness of the idea in the content gives diffusion its special character" (2003: 5–6).

Design anthropology emerged as a "new idea" sometime around 2000,[15] the invention being "a hybrid approach that combines insights and practices from design and anthropology" (Halse, 2008). However, the idea had already been incubating for some time in multiple locations. For example, by the 1990s, design firms like IDEO[16] and Doblin were using interdisciplinary project teams that included designers and anthropologists.[17] Having been introduced to multiple social groups through communication channels that included conference presentations,[18] published articles, projects, dissertations, and academic courses, the term was well established by 2011 when the first edited book (event #11) was published.

According to Rogers, the innovation-development process begins with the identification of a problem or unmet need followed by *research and development, commercialization* or *scaling, diffusion and adoption*, and *consequences* (Rogers, 2003: 137). Halse (2008: 3) described "the basic problem" that design anthropologists aim to solve as "that of linking interesting ethnographic observation with an interesting design suggestion." The 12 events in our analysis are strong indicators that *research and development* in design anthropological theory and practice are ongoing. Examples presented in Table 4.3 provide evidence of scaling, diffusion, and adoption of design anthropology by individuals and institutions. Although it is too soon to do more than speculate about the consequences of diffusion and adoption, there are already interesting developments as both design and anthropology attempt to redraw their boundaries. Christian Madsbjerg's provocative presentation at the EPIC conference in 2014 asked attendees to "divorce design." Referring to the "marriage between ethnography and design," Madsbjerg argued that although some companies had developed "thoughtful design research models," other designers "disinterested in true ethnography but cognizant of its widespread appeal adopted a watered-down version."[19] In tandem with cautionary advice, other consequences include the introduction of focused academic programs and courses.

Homophily and Heterophily

Homophily and heterophily are relevant concepts in understanding the diffusion of new ideas, specifically, the dissemination of information about design anthropology. Homophily refers to the tendency to associate and bond with people who are most like us, for example, people who are similar in age, gender, occupation, or educational background. Physical and social proximity can also engender homophily. The well-known idiom "birds of a feather flock together" describes homophilous social groups. Communication within a homophilous social group – between individuals who share common meanings, beliefs, and understandings – tends to be more effective, efficient, and rewarding. Heterophily, on the other hand, relates to difference and diversity. Being the opposite of homophily, heterophily is defined "as the degree to which pairs of individuals who interact are different in certain attributes" (Rogers, 2003: 6). Due to differences in social status, language, and a range of other factors, heterophilous communication between dissimilar individuals can result in cognitive dissonance when they are confronted with messages that contradict their existing belief systems.

The differences between homophilous communication and heterophilous communication have a major impact on the spread of new ideas. Rogers notes that "the communication of new ideas is likely to have greater effects in terms of knowledge gain, attitude formation and change, and overt behavior change" (2003: 19). Although this would seem to have a positive impact on diffusion, homophily presents "an invisible barrier to the flow of innovations within a system" (2003:306). Communicating with others who do not share our language or the meanings we assign to things and experiences can be difficult and frustrating, especially when attempting to communicate new ideas. In communicating "the New" to heterophilous groups within organizational settings, Erwin (2014) writes that,

> One of the biggest challenges in creating the New is to make it understandable to others and, not incidentally, to oneself. The challenge of clarifying new discoveries or concepts to organizational stakeholders – many of whom are not part of the development phase – is a notorious gap in the internal adoption and implementation of new ideas.
>
> *(2014: 3)*

Despite the challenges in communication, heterophilous networks often connect different social groups or "cliques." When two individuals form links, or "bridges" (Granovetter, 1973), between heterophilous social groups, information about innovations can be conveyed and spread to more people. In our analysis, we found that three individuals from Group A (event #11) serve as liaisons that bridge Group A and Group C, two networks that might not otherwise be connected (Figure 4.6). Rogers argued that "the very nature of diffusion demands at least some degree of heterophily between the two participants" (2003: 306).

> Homophily accelerates the diffusion process, but limits the spread of an innovation to those individuals connected in a close-knit network. Ultimately, the diffusion process can only occur through communication links that are at least somewhat heterophilous.

Network analysis of the 12 events that occurred between 2011 and 2016 suggests that information explicitly related to design anthropology is being communicated through mostly homophilous networks. While this bodes well for the *research and development* phase of the innovation process, it does not indicate that information about design anthropological practice and knowledge of its theory is broadly diffusing to heterophilous networks. New ideas are inherently unstable, which makes it challenging to communicate them. We considered whether there is consensus among those who were identified as Core Contributors (i.e., the COIN) to take a slow and steady approach that builds a substantial body of knowledge, attracting people who share the values of collaborative participation and collective creativity, and are willing and able to contribute to developing theory and practice. This would be lost if massive promotional efforts and commercialization were a priority. The conscious scaffolding of common ground and shared language suggests a deliberate, if not explicit, decision to solidify the core principles and values that underpin design anthropological theory and practice as opposed to promoting it as the next silver bullet that promises to reveal the wants and unmet needs of "users."

Attributes of Innovation

Another relevant concept from Diffusion Theory is what Rogers identified as the five attributes of innovation: *relative advantage, compatibility, complexity, trialability, and observability* (2003: 223). We can apply these attributes as a lens to examine how each factor is weighed and how it affects the decision-making process. What is the *advantage* or benefit of adopting the design anthropological approach relative to other forms of qualitative field work that incorporate design and ethnography? How *compatible* is design anthropological methodology with someone's current work? This consideration is not only about a person's individual work, but also concerns whether the "new idea" will be accepted as a validated form of inquiry in their primary social group, in other words, by their colleagues. *Complexity* relates to the multidimensional nature of new ideas. For example, does it require new hardware or software? Does it require the acquisition of new knowledge? How difficult is it to learn to apply this new approach in current projects? The next attribute is *trialability*. Is design anthropology accessible or *"tryable?"* Can it be tried at a low cost in a low-risk situation or environment? Finally, is design anthropology *observable*? How does someone come to know it exists? Can people observe it being practiced or see the results of design anthropological practice?

As an emerging field, design anthropology currently receives low scores on the attributes. Outside of anthropology and design the field is literally unknown. Even within these disciplines, opportunities to learn about or observe design anthropology are limited to a few books, articles, and conferences. The diffusion of design anthropological theory and practice will depend on increasing opportunities for observing and trying, and for evaluating its relative advantage, complexity, and compatibility with current approaches, practices, and mind sets. We can collectively imagine the possibilities, collaborations, and participations in how this might unfold.

Conclusion

In this chapter we have presented a snapshot of the characteristics, status, and diffusion of design anthropological theory and practice. Using the criteria of the *WoS*, we began by establishing that design anthropology is not a formally recognized "subject area." However, through a series of Web-based searches and using Google Ngram and Scholar, we found that it meets a broad set of generally recognized indicators (see Table 4.5), substantiating the claim that design anthropology is an emerging field of knowledge production.

We then conducted an analysis of a set of 12 significant events (Table 4.3) between 2011 and 2016 that were explicitly associated with design anthropology and the 180 people (i.e., Contributors) who contributed to them. We converted the events and people into a node and link list for SNA. Using the network analysis tool MultiNet/Negopy, we identified three distinct clusters (Figure 4.4), one of which was isolated from the others. The group of 19 Contributors (Table 4.4) to event number 11 included 16 people who did not participate in any of the other 11 events and three who served as bridges or liaisons from Group A to Group C (Figure 4.6). Group C includes the 13 individuals who occupy the most central positions in the network of 180 Contributors to the 12 events. We identify these 13 individuals as "Core Contributors." The third cluster, Group B, includes individuals who contributed to only one of the remaining 11 events clustered in Group C.

We also analyzed 27 institutions that were associated with the group of Core Contributors, individuals who were either members of the Research Network for Design Anthropology Steering Group or listed as a Network Participant. Using Google Sites, we identified the number of hits for the phrase "Website URL AND 'design anthropology'" (Figure 4.7). The results show that 61percent of the hits came from five URLs, four of which are institutional websites. The fifth is the website for EPIC People, indicating strong support for the topic of design anthropology.

Network analysis exists as an abstraction without overlaying the dimension of context. Consequently, we applied three conceptual/theoretical frameworks related to collaboration, collective intelligence, innovation networks, and the diffusion of innovation to our findings. Applying the COIN model (Figure 4.8), we identified an ecosystem comprised of the Core Contributor group, a CLN of individuals who contributed to two or more events, and a larger CIN. Through collaborative engagement, creative improvisation and innovation, and direct communication, we suggest that the resulting CKN acts as a feedback loop to further knowledge production and the development of design anthropological theory and practice.

We described how design anthropology embodies the characteristics of an expanding CoP through the mutual engagement among Contributors, collective negotiation, and the development of a growing repertoire of resources. We suggested how the concepts of peripherality and marginality frame issues around *participation* in the 12 events, and suggest implications for evolving networks and communities over time.

Finally, we applied Diffusion Theory to explain how information about design anthropology is being communicated through various channels (i.e., the 12 events) and shared through multiple networks. We described how the four main elements of Diffusion Theory – the invention or idea, communication channels, social systems, and adoption over time – relate to our data and how the five attributes of innovation can be applied to predict if and how rapidly the innovation that is design anthropology might diffuse.

The diffusion of design anthropological theory and practice through multiple channels and networks suggests implications for the rapid expansion of design's scope and relevance, and the radical overhaul that Murphy and Marcus (2013) described as the "rebuilding of the anthropological apparatus." We invite our readers to be the judge: is design anthropology growing or contracting? Or will it be subsumed as an interest group or subtrack by another research community? Will it continue to develop within regionalized networks with a few bridges serving as liaisons? The decision to distinguish design anthropology as a distinct field of knowledge production signals a recognition of its unique value, and that efforts to keep up the momentum are worthwhile. It implies that we need a collective mind to pursue this research agenda.

Notes

1 Thomson Reuters' *Web of Science* (accessed July 12, 2016), http://ipscience.thomson-reuters.com/.
2 Google Ngram (accessed July 12, 2016), https://books.google.com/ngrams.
3 Data is continuously being added. These searches on Google Scholar were conducted on July 12, 2016.
4 ProQuest (accessed on July 8, 2016), www.proquest.com/.
5 Dissertation and thesis searches on Google Scholar and ProQuest conducted on July 12, 2016.
6 When using Web-based tools, the results will vary depending on factors such as the time and date of the search. The results presented in this chapter are not intended to

provide a definitive analysis. Instead they provide a method for making sense of the vast amount of data available on the Internet.

7 Gunn, Otto, and Smith presented a paper entitled "Design Anthropology: Intertwining Different Timelines, Scales and Movements," at the 11th Biennial EASA Association of Social Anthropologists Conference (Maynooth, Ireland, August 2010), Although this could be considered a significant event, it was not included because the paper was revised and included in the edited volume, *Design Anthropology: Theory and Practice* (Gunn, Otto, & Smith, 2013). Another publication, *Design and Anthropology* (Gunn and Donovan, 2012) could also be considered for this list.

8 "Anthrodesign" is a Yahoo group formed in 2002 by Natalie Hanson. It currently has an international membership of over 2000+ anthropologists, designers, and ethnographers. (accessed July 28, 2016), http://anthrodesign.com.

9 The Design Anthropology panel (number 10) is an exception since the list of presenters is available to AAA annual meeting attendees. I acquired permission to include the names of these presenters.

10 Network analysis is a multidisciplinary field. Terms are often different in its application in various fields. For example, "nodes" can be called "actors," and "links" can be called "edges."

11 Eigenvector is a term used in linear algebra to describe the linear transformation T from vector space V over a field F. The term is also used in network analysis.

12 The names of Steering Committee members and network participants are listed on the KADK webpage for the Research Network for Design Anthropology, https://kadk.dk/en/who-network.

13 The complete list of URLs and the search results are available on the companion website for the book.

14 Twelve Interactive Exhibitions, Design Anthropological Futures Conference website (accessed July 27, 2016), https://kadk.dk/sites/default/files/downloads/article/interactive_exhibitions_documentation_002.pdf.

15 Halse wrote that "a number of anthropologists working with or in design practice formed a group in 2001." By 2008 this group had 40 members. He notes that "It is not a research forum nor a network of practitioners, but something in between. Under the label 'design anthropology,' we meet regularly to establish a kind of middle ground and discuss issues that cut across the traditional divide between academia and industry" (2008: 7–8).

16 IDEO's famous Shopping Cart concept (accessed on July 27, 2016), www.ideo.com/work/shopping-cart-concept.

17 Rick E. Robinson, Doblin's research director during this time, and design lead, John Cain, were instrumental in these early explorations. Robinson went on to found other design firms including E-Lab in 1994 and later Iota Partners with John Cain in 2010.

18 Halse wrote that "concern with *participation* and *qualitative field methods*" was addressed in the field of participatory design (PD) and as a topic at PD conferences. He adds that the annual Ethnographic Praxis in Industry Conference (EPIC) founded in 2005, provided another venue for discussions on ethnography and design in or with commercial settings (2008: 7).

19 "Happy Birthday, Now Grown Up" (video and transcript accessed July 27, 2016), www.epicpeople.org/happy-birthday-now-grow-up/.

References

Barnett, H.G. 1953. *Innovation: The Basis of Cultural Change*. New York: McGraw-Hill.

Clark, Brandon. 2008. *Design as Sociopolitical Navigation: A Performative Framework for Action-Oriented Design*. Ph.D. dissertation, University of Southern Denmark, Odense, Denmark.

Clarke, Alison (Ed.). 2010. *Design Anthropology: Object Culture for the 21st Century*. Vienna: Springer.

Erwin, Kim. 2014. *Communicating the New: Methods to Shape and Accelerate Innovation*. Hoboken, NJ: Wiley.

Gladwell, Malcom. 2000. *The Tipping Point: How Little Things Can Make a Big Difference*. New York: Little, Brown and Company.

Gloor, Peter. 2006. *Swarm Creativity*. New York: Oxford University Press.

Granovetter, Mark S. 1973. The Strength of Weak Ties. *American Journal of Sociology*, 78, 1360–1380.

Gunn, Wendy and Jared Donovan. 2012. *Design and Anthropology*. Burlington, VT: Ashgate Publishing.

Gunn, Wendy, Ton Otto, and Rachel C. Smith. 2010. *Design Anthropology: Intertwining Different Timelines, Scales and Movements*. Paper Presented at the 11th Biennial EASA European Association of Social Anthropologist Conference, Maynooth, Ireland.

Gunn, Wendy, Ton Otto, and Rachel C. Smith (Eds.). 2013. *Design Anthropology: Theory and Practice*. New York: Bloomsbury.

Halse, Joachim. 2008. Design Anthropology: Borderland Experiments with Participation, Performance and Situated Intervention. Ph.D. dissertation, IT University of Copenhagen, Copenhagen, Denmark.

Jara, Elisa. 2011. COIN Model. Graphic Illustration. Savannah College of Art and Design, Savannah, GA.

Kjaersgaard, Mette. 2011. *Between the Actual and the Potential: The Challenges of Design Anthropology*. Ph.D. dissertation, Aarhaus University, Copenhagen, Denmark.

Lave, Jean and Etienne Wenger. 1991. *Situated Learning: Legitimate Peripheral Participation*. Cambridge: Cambridge University Press.

Leydesdorff, Loett, Stephen Carley, and Ismael Rofols. 2013. Global Maps of Science Based on the New Web of Science Categories. *Sociometrics*, 94, 589–593.

Murphy, Kevin and George Marcus. 2013. Epilogue: Ethnography and Design, Ethnography in Design...Ethnography by Design. In W. Gunn, T. Otto, and R.C. Smith (Eds.), *Design Anthropology: Theory and Practice*, 251–267. New York: Bloomsbury.

O'Toole, Robert. 2015. *Fit, Stick, Spread and Grow: Transdisciplinary Design Thinking for the Remaking of Higher Education*. Ph.D. dissertation, University of Warwick, Coventry, UK.

Otto, Ton and Rachel C. Smith. 2013. Design Anthropology: A Distinct Way of Kowing. In W. Gunn, T. Otto, and R.S. Smith (Eds.), *Design Anthropology: Theory and Practice*, 1–32. New York: Bloomsbury.

Pedersen, Jens. 2007. *Protocols of Research and Design: Reflections on a Participatory Design Project (sort of)*. Ph.D. dissertation, IT University of Copenhagen, Copenhagen, Denmark.

Porter, Alan and Ismael Rafols. 2009. Is Science Becoming More Interdisciplinary? Measuring and Mapping Six Research Fields Over Time. *Sociometrics*, 81(3), 719–745.

Rogers, Everett. 2003. *Diffusion of Innovations* (5th Ed.). New York: Free Press.

Shade, Molly. 2015. *The Burner Project: Privacy and Social Control in a Networked World*. M.S. thesis, University of North Texas, Denton, TX.

Smith, Rachel C., Kasper Tang Vangkilde, Mette G. Kjaersgaard, Ton Otto, Joachim Halse, and Thomas Binder (Eds.). 2016. *Design Anthropological Futures*. New York: Bloomsbury.

Wenger, Etienne. 1999. *Communities of Practice: Learning, Meaning, and Identity*. New York: Cambridge University Press.

5

EPILOGUE

Final Thoughts...For Now

In the time that it has taken to research and write this book, design anthropology has continued to evolve as a transdisciplinary field that brings together design's fundamental orientation to change, and critical anthropological observation and analysis. The purpose of this book has been to go beyond the earlier goal to describe "ethnographically informed design" that characterized the first encounters between designers and anthropologists, and instead to explore design anthropology as a distinct "style of knowing" (Otto & Smith, 2013). This final chapter offers concluding observations that are intended to provoke further discussion about the emerging field of design anthropology, and the networks and communities that nurture and support its ongoing development.

Chaos and Emergent Order

Design anthropology is part of a broad movement of disciplinary convergence that is creating the potential for *disorder* by disrupting disciplinary boundaries and *new order* through the emergence of hybridized fields of knowledge production. Douglas (2002) reminds us that although disorder creates chaos by perturbing established patterns and routines, it also has "indefinite creative potential." For this reason, Douglas argues that we do not condemn disorder but instead recognize that "It symbolizes both danger and power" (2002: 117).

A Field in Its Own Right

Design anthropology is an emerging field in its own right. Its transdisciplinary nature – the fact that it engages many disciplines – makes it impossible to fit neatly as a subfield of anthropology or a sub-subfield of business anthropology. It is not the anthropology *of* design proposed by Suchman (2011: 3). Although practiced in many different ways, design anthropology has come to represent a distinctive approach to future-making characterized by "inclusive, collective, and public approaches" (Pelle, Nilsson, & Topgaard, 2014) that focus on "dynamic situations and social relations." Rather than looking to the creation of "new" things as the drivers of social and economic change, design anthropology looks instead to the improvisations that occur in everyday activities as people "create and transform their environments" (Gunn, Otto, & Smith, 2010).

Not to Be Confused with Design Ethnography

Design anthropology should not be confused with "design ethnography" or "ethnographic design"[1] which focus on engagements between ethnographers (who might or might not be anthropologists), designers, and design researchers. Conversations about "ethnographic design" raise questions about the nature of ethnography and the misuse of the term as synonymous with fieldwork. Ingold (2014) referred to the persistent blurring of the distinction between "ethnography," which is literally defined as *"writing about people"* (2014: 385), and "participant observation" – documented encounters with others in the process of field research. Ingold argues that conflating ethnography and participant observation "is doing great harm" to anthropology (2014: 383). The pervasive misappropriation of the term within anthropology and beyond suggests that it may have completely broken loose from its moorings (2014: 383), that it is too late to unscramble the egg. However, Ingold's admonition deserves special consideration here in light of what he calls the "temporal distortion that contrives to render the aftermath of our meetings with people as their anterior condition." He writes that,

> to cast encounters as ethnographic is to consign the incipient – the about-to-happen in unfolding relationships – to the temporal past already over. It is as though, on meeting others face-to-face, one's back is already turned to them. This is to leave behind those who, in the moment of encounter, stand before.
>
> *(2014: 386)*

Design anthropology is the antithesis of this depiction of ethnography by virtue of its persistent focus on the dynamic, *incipient moments* as the crucible in which transformative change is brewing. Framed as "ethnographies of the possible" (Halse, 2013), design anthropology ameliorates the difference in temporal orientation between anthropology and design, while at the same time, returns ethnography to its original meaning.

Parallel Trajectories

Two regional clusters represent parallel trajectories in design anthropology. One trajectory is centered in Denmark and is supported by a network of dedicated scholar-practitioners who explicitly aim to develop design anthropology as a unique form of knowledge production and further a research agenda through collaboration and collective engagement. A second trajectory in the United States is less focused. Most of the United States-based researchers have ties to the Denmark-centered network.

Established communities such as the Participatory Design (PD) Conference and the Ethnographic Praxis in Industry Conference (EPIC), and its associated website EPIC People (www.epicpeople.org/about-epic/) have served as forums for the work of design anthropologists. It is possible that the nascent field might eventually be subsumed by one or both of these conference communities. It is too soon to tell if there is sufficient energy and commitment to propel design anthropology out of the orbit of these well-established groups.

Technological Challenges

Many examples of design anthropology involve grounded field work within relatively small groups and communities and contexts. How will design anthropologists respond to continuously changing technologies that pose a direct challenge to *in situ* field research? For example, an increasingly instrumented world and the ubiquitous presence of sensors pose a direct challenge to conventional field research. Iota + Sapient Nitro,[2] a pioneering research consultancy, is helping firms experiment with using sensors to continuously collect data, leveraging the Internet of Things (IoT) to bridge "the 'last mile' between big data and daily life."

There is no way to know exactly how the future will unfold as change continuously ripples through the complex assemblages of the contemporary world (Ong and Collier, 2005). Attempts to "understand 'users'" by cobbling together methods and tools of anthropology and design have been exhausted. The promise of design anthropology is that we can build on our collective experience to create and continually improvise ways in which we not only observe, but *see* the potential in the myriad pathways that are opening moment by moment in daily life. The challenge to shape and transform what is, to envision what might be lies beyond our current notion of human-centered design.

Notes

1 Ethnography and Design: Mutual Provocations (October 2016) was organized by CoLED, "an interdisciplinary hub for innovative research on the future of ethnography and design." CoLED is an initiative of the University of California system that was inspired by George Marcus' ethnographic "Design Studios" and Paul Rabinow's "Collaboratories." http://coled.ucsd.edu.

2 Iota Partners and Sapeint + Nitro (accessed August 3, 2016). www.iota-partners. com/; www.sapientnitro.com/en-us.html#home.

References

Douglas, Mary. 2002. *Purity and Danger: An Analysis of Concepts of Pollution and Taboo.* London: Routledge.

Ehn, Pelle, Elisabet M. Nilsson, and Richard Topgaard. 2014. Introduction. In Pelle Ehn, Elisabet M. Nilsson, and Richard Topgaard (Eds.), *Making Futures: Marginal Notes on Innovation, Design, and Democracy*, 1–13. Cambridge, MA: MIT Press.

Gunn, Wendy, Ton Otto, and Rachel C. Smith. 2010. Design Anthropology: Intertwining Different Timelines, Scales and Movements. 11th Biennial EASA European Association of Social Anthropologists Conference, Maynooth, Ireland, August 2010.

Halse, Joachim. 2013. Ethnographies of the Possible. In Wendy Gunn, Ton Otto, and Rachel Charlotte Smith (Eds.), *Design Anthropology: Theory and Practice*, 180–196. New York: Bloomsbury.

Ingold, Tim. 2014. That's Enough About Ethnography! *HAU: Journal of Ethnographic Theory*, 4(1), 383–395.

Ong, Aihwa and Stephen J. Collier (Eds.). 2005. *Global Assemblages: Technology, Politics, and Ethics as Anthropological Problems.* Malden, MA: Blackwell Publishing.

Otto, Ton and Rachel C. Smith. 2013. Design Anthropology: A Distinct Way of Knowing. In Wendy Gunn, Ton Otto, and Rachel Charlotte Smith (Eds.), *Design Anthropology: Theory and Practice*, 1–29. New York: Bloomsbury.

Suchman, Lucy. 2011. Anthropological Relocations and the Limits of Design. *Annual Review of Anthropology*, 40, 1–18.

INDEX

Locators in **bold** refer to tables, those in *italic* refer to figures while those containing 'n' refer to notes.

Made in United States
North Haven, CT
18 July 2022

21541187R00072